GENTLY
DOWN THE
STREAM

A collection of columns
by **St. Louis-Post-Dispatch** columnist

BILL McCLELLAN

CREDITS

Copy editor • Frank Reust

Illustrator • Dan Martin

Designer • Wade Wilson

Sales & Marketing • Cory Parolin-Doehler and Angie Clark

Special thanks to Doug Weaver of Kansas City Star Books

© 2010 St. Louis Post-Dispatch Books
All rights reserved. No part of this book may be reproduced, stored in a retrieval system or transmitted in any form or by any means electronic, mechanical, photocopying, recording or otherwise without the prior consent of the publisher.

Softcover
ISBN 9780-9842084-4-9

Printed by Walsworth Publishing Co., Marceline, Mo.

To order additional copies:
Call 1-877-767-8785 or go to www.thepost-dispatchstore.com

GENTLY DOWN THE STREAM

A collection of columns
by **St. Louis-Post-Dispatch** columnist
BILL McCLELLAN

CONTENTS

9	Preface by Bill McClellan
11	Dedication
13	Miss Mac's turn to make a family
16	Man is making a home under Jefferson Avenue bridge
19	A cheeseburger with a side of justice
22	'Angel' of a refugee is tested by hard times
25	Foster child makes good; mother of 3 adopts 3 more
27	When a storm of words goes to court, delay can be kind
30	Eccentric lives, 'art' are siblings' legacy
33	War on drugs is a hard sell when justice is a casualty
35	Wee folk can't spin magic like that of dad and daughter
38	Social gaffe is really an act of kindness in disguise
41	The voice on the other end of the line has a real life, and feelings, too
43	Black cat winds up costing a lot of green
46	Saloon owner's glory days went up in flames
48	Did fantasy, rum and coke spark fire at saloon?
50	Trial is reminder: Sometimes, nice people do stupid things
52	With Medium Mac, suspend disbelief
55	A family's Titanic miracle lives on
58	Child pornography cases: Measuring the time for the crime
61	Uninsured woman got top care, then got arrested
64	Free coffee, free news, but these policies cost us

67	Lead in soil: Hazard or sustenance?
70	How close a shameful memory was to a tragedy
72	Passport shop thrives out of step
75	You can have insurance and still end up $90,000 in debt
78	Man who wasn't really her father may have left a legacy
81	Lutheran pastors answer the Call
84	'Interacting' lets passive folks be aggressive
87	Young historian shed light on Vietnam
90	You talking to me? Then please quit whispering
93	Name game nearly backfires on man held on forgery charge
95	From Cuba, with love: No dictating what heart knows
98	Murder may be key to drug dealer's cell
101	A deal is struck, then death throws a curve
104	Practical? No, but cat and boy make a Christmas connection
106	Institution to home, to grave: Otto, RIP
108	What's 2 weeks in the county jail to a fellow who is lucky in love?
110	Lots of history in one little house
113	Next election, let's all elect
115	The story of how my car went the way of TV tubes
119	Kindnesses lift one up in a series of downs
122	Business leadership style steals success from St. Louis
125	Family anchor has dispensed discipline, faith and love
127	Drug war casualty stirs more reflection
130	Farm girl feared cows but became early riser
133	Cueto suit paints me as a guy with power
136	Watching dreams unravel
139	Town rallies for immigrant teen chasing dream
142	True story: Woman was mobster's daughter
145	Family-owned business greases gears of history
148	Strangers give man new hope, then fate steps in
151	Daughter isn't buying theory about empty roads
154	Overweight? Nah, just a high body mass index
156	High hopes for son ... and a family's loss
159	Why are these guys on corporate boards?

162	Prof enjoys debate, rocking the boat
164	Something didn't add up in boardinghouse assault
167	When it comes to family, we're all business
170	Anyone selling a bridge? 'Cause I've hit the jackpot
173	Two men's lives: Success stories from a checkered past
175	Eviction notice adds to plight of transgender county resident
177	A wartime love lost, but never forgotten
180	Two ill men's paths cross on S. Grand
183	For piano tuner, it's the busiest time of the year
186	Child porn ensares adopter of children
189	Seasons fly by in the blink of an eye
191	The evolution of newspapers can be traced to two meteors
194	Death, crime mark shift in small town
197	'Lieutenant Blues' always seemed to find his man
200	Changes are shaking up a simple life
202	Mental illness, family tie complicate murder trial
205	What would jury say in beauty vs. A-B?
208	A lifetime of brightening lives brought joy into volunteer's heart
211	Changing times: Now not sparing the rod leads to a day in court
214	Investigator has his eye out for cheaters
217	St. Louis is truly something special
220	Dad's investment was pie in the sky
223	Motive for murder may never be known
226	The very rich need to hear that they'll be seen as chintzy
228	Like aromas from a bakery, memories of a good life linger
230	Judge declines to swallow story of man who sold other's goods
232	Is civilization in decline? You bet; look at racetracks
234	Even lawyers stung by 'evolving' economy
236	Even at the end, Orthwein kept his Old Money values
239	Country clubs love a little socialism
242	Neighborhood's long history could be overwhelmed by development
245	A letter, long ago, for Miss Mildred
248	About the author

PREFACE

7.21.2010

An astute reader once pointed out that a great many of my columns seem to concern the end of things -- the shutting down of businesses (mostly taverns) and the deaths of people. Why do I dwell on ends rather than beginnings?

Because it is easier to recognize an end than to spot a beginning.

Had I been writing a newspaper column in Philadelphia in October 1723, I would have been writing about anything except the arrival in that city of young Benjamin Franklin. How would I have known that Franklin was going to become who he became?

But the death of a prominent soap-maker? The closing of a popular public house? These are the things that someone with even limited vision can recognize.

I mention this because a number of columns in this collection are about the end of things. Some of the people whose ends are herein chronicled are people I knew not at all. Others were well-known to me. Like Lino Gambaro, the patriarch of the Missouri Baking Company. I met him years ago when I went into his bakery and bought a lump of pizza dough. "How long do I let it rise?" I asked. "Do you drink?" he responded. "Yes," I said. "Two beers. Let it rise for two beers," he said.

Or John Brophy, who managed the newsroom for years. Once I complained that as a longtime columnist, I deserved a desk near a window. I was tired of looking at the walls. I wanted a view. The next day, on the wall in front of my desk, hung an electrically lighted scene of a waterfall. It probably came from a tavern that had just shut down.

Actually, most of the columns in this book are not about ends. Most are harder to classify. They're just stories. That is, after all, what I do -- tell stories. It is an enjoyable way to make a living. I spend most of my time gathering material, and then I come back to the newspaper, gaze at the waterfall on the wall, and write something. It does not sound like work, does it? It really isn't.

What was work was selecting columns for this book. Needless to say, I had no objective standards. I read all of the columns I have written in the four years since the last collection of columns was published. Then I read them again. Generally, I found that on the second reading, I liked the ones I had not liked on the first reading. Perhaps I should have asked for somebody else's opinion. But I didn't. I just grabbed a bunch that I found interesting. Some of them were not necessarily popular with readers. In fact, a couple of them were decidedly unpopular.

Also, I decided to include a couple of two-part stories and even a three-part series on a trial. One of the two-parters is about Noe Guzman, a young man from New Haven who decided to join the Marine Corps and learned, to his astonishment, that he was an illegal alien. That was the first part. The second part was about how the town reacted to the news. The other two-parter is about Alan Milburn, a cocaine dealer who was doing a life sentence in federal prison when he got a chance to get out of prison if he would agree to testify against the man who had long ago killed his girlfriend. He agreed to testify, but the alleged murderer died before the trial.

The three-parter is the story of an arson trial. As regular readers know, I enjoy writing about trials as they unfold. It is interesting to write a story when you don't know how that story will end. The defendant in this trial was accused of setting fire to her tavern.

By the way, I liked her. That seems to be one of my flaws. I like people whom many readers don't. Then again, I like to think that the strength of many of these stories is that the heroes are themselves flawed.

Nobody's perfect. But those of you who continue to read newspapers are close to perfect. As a newspaper columnist, I thank you, and I hope that you like at least some of the columns included herein.

Meanwhile, remember the old song — merrily, merrily, merrily, life is but a dream.

DEDICATION

To **John Michael McGuire**, a great reporter and a better friend

MISS MAC'S TURN TO MAKE A FAMILY

4.4.2010

In September 1989, I walked my daughter to her first day of kindergarten. I remember something akin to sadness when the bell rang and Lorna ran into the school. I understood that I had begun to lose her.

Thirteen years later, I helped her move into a dormitory at the University of Illinois. I did fine on the drive to Urbana, but not so well when I started to carry her things up the stairs and into her room. Among the things was a bulletin board with photos of the family – my wife, my son, the dogs and me. Within hours, we would be reduced to photographs. Her life without us was taking shape. I started to cry.

"It's okay, Dad," she said.

"Get hold of yourself," said my wife.

Four years later, I drove with Lorna to northern California. She had joined Teach for America and would be teaching high school biology in Richmond. We drove past the school. It had a rough look. I worried.

A year later, I visited her classroom. She was known as Miss Mac. To my eye, she was hardly older than her students, but she was clearly in charge and seemed comfortable. She was an adult. I was taken by surprise.

Last month, she got married. The ceremony was in the backyard of my wife's youngest sister. My wife and her sister did all the work. My job was to walk Lorna from the house to the garden. I was standing on the patio when she came out of the living room. She looked stunning. Young women in love so often are.

She tilted her head and smiled. "Don't make me cry," she said. I shook my head, as if to say, "Don't worry." I heard one of my wife's sisters say, "Look, he's crying already."

Arm in arm, we walked toward the garden.

Behind us, on the roof of the house, the groom, Darryl Sanchez, had set up a computer so the ceremony could be seen in his native Nicaragua. He has an older brother in Managua. He has friends and family in El Viejo, a small town near Chinandega.

Darryl and his mother, Miriam, came to this country from El Viejo 10 years ago. Darryl's father, Manuel, was already here.

We had dinner at their house a couple of nights before the wedding. Miriam cooked fish. Manuel brought out a bottle of Nicaraguan rum. Manuel likes baseball. He likes baseball so much that he named his second son after New York Mets slugger Darryl Strawberry.

I am a Cubs fan and I would have preferred Manuel to have named his second son Ryne Sanchez, or Ernie Sanchez, or even Sammy Sanchez, but as my wife tells me about so many things, "This is not about you."

With the people in El Viejo and Managua watching, I walked Lorna to the garden. Darryl stepped forward. We shook hands and then embraced. Lorna and Darryl then turned toward the young man who was to conduct the ceremony. His name is Rishi Patel. He teaches math at Richmond High. He received his divinity credentials through the Internet. He was holding a book. Inside the book was the ceremony he was to read.

He began reading. I recognized it. It was the ceremony I wrote for my wedding 30 years ago.

I glanced over at my father-in-law to see if he recognized it. He was not enamored of it 30 years ago. That's because I gave the ceremony a dramatic twist. When the preacher said, "If anybody knows why these two should not be joined in Holy Matrimony, let him speak now or forever hold his peace," I had a friend stand up and say, "It's not that I'm against marriage, but these two have been living together and seem happy so I don't see the point."

Our families did not know that was coming, so everybody gasped. But the preacher waited only a second and then talked about the commitment we were making and so on, and people realized the interruption had been part of the ceremony. Still, a lot of people thought it was tacky.

Lorna and Darryl opted for a more traditional approach. The moment came to object, and no one did. I was glad.

The young men and the young women in the wedding party could have come from Central Casting. They were handsome and beautiful and diverse – Latinos, whites, a black, a Jew and, of course, an Indian reading the ceremony. The people watching in Nicaragua probably thought, "The beer commercials are true."

I sat there and I thought, "How did I get here?"

It's a question I have asked myself frequently, and the answer is always the same. My family brought me.

I hope my daughter will be as happy as I've been.

MAN IS MAKING A HOME
UNDER JEFFERSON AVENUE BRIDGE

12.14.2008

Dan Zuroweste is the superintendent of Gershenson Construction, the man in charge of building the new Jefferson Avenue bridge. Last fall, as he prepared to knock down the old bridge, he discovered a small colony of people living under it. He told them he was about to demolish the bridge and they would have to leave. Most picked up their belongings and left.

But one of the squatters had more than just a sleeping bag and some cardboard. His name was Robert and he had a house. It was roughly constructed out of plywood, but it was still a house. Robert told Zuroweste that he had been living under the bridge for about 12 years. He was polite and seemingly resigned to his fate. You have to do what you have to do, he said to the construction boss.

It was to Robert's great fortune that Zuroweste's nickname is "Hippie," and the nickname is only partly due to Zuroweste's long hair. He has a big job with considerable authority, but he retains a certain live and let live attitude. "I'm good-natured," is the way he describes himself.

He checked with the businesses on Chouteau Avenue whose property adjoins the bridge. The businesses did not have a problem with Robert.

So Zuroweste had his construction workers move Robert's house to the side when they demolished the bridge. When they built the new one, they moved Robert's house back under it.

I visited Robert on Friday. I approached his house. It's about 20 feet tall. There is no ground-level entrance. The entrance is about 10 feet above the ground. Robert uses a ladder to get in and out. He can pull the ladder in after he's up. It's a security precaution.

Robert said he is 45. I didn't ask about his past. Over the years, I've learned that it's difficult, almost impossible, to verify old stories, anyway. Suffice it to say that it is a complicated and generally sad path that leads a man to a life under a bridge.

Not that Robert is alone in that lifestyle. After a few minutes of small talk, we set off down the railroad tracks to the next bridge. A man lives under that one, too. He lives in the open air. Robert said he'd come across an extra coat and he thought the man might need it.

"He's your story," said Robert. "Me, it's like I'm cheating with what I have. This man has almost nothing. Just a little camp."

As we walked, Robert told me he was a Christian. Not necessarily a church-going Christian, but a believer, and consequently, an optimist. "Jesus was an optimist," Robert said. He said he was a musician. He played the guitar and the piano. He said he'd done some roofing for a while. He said he knew basic carpentry. He said the authorities knew he was living under the bridge, but he was still concerned that anything I might write could force their hand. I had thought of that, too, but there I was, anyway.

When we neared the next bridge, Robert said that the proper way to do this would be to yell out a greeting before we reached the man's camp. You don't want to just walk up on him. You don't want to meddle, Robert said. I'm a professional meddler, I said. Yes, said Robert.

The man had a small fire going. "Hey, I got a coat!" Robert yelled. The man waved his arms at us. "I don't need it!" he shouted. Robert put it on the ground, and we turned and headed back up the tracks to his place.

Robert has a smaller structure behind his house. It's his shower room. He has a small propane heater he uses to heat water. He told me it's important to keep clean.

In fact, one of the day's first chores is always to get water. He has several gallon jugs. He put them in a bag and tied that to a large plastic bag that he uses to collect aluminum cans, and we set off down the tracks again. He said there are businesses that don't mind him using their faucets to get water. We went to one such business, filled the jugs and headed back down the tracks.

He told me the railroad detectives know about his camp but leave him alone because he never steals anything. In fact, he keeps things clean.

I asked if he ever thought about hopping on a slow-moving freight and heading south for the winter. No, he said. The weather might sound better, but wherever you went would be new. You wouldn't know your way around, he said. Here, I've got my necessities, he said – a place to stay, food.

He said he sometimes goes in to the various agencies around downtown that feed people, but more often, he can take care of himself in that regard. He's a scrapper, collecting cans, and he begs. He has a sign that reads, God Bless You, and he sometimes walks or takes the bus to the western edge of the city, and sits there with his sign.

All in all, it's a hard life. There is not much lying around. It takes as much effort to survive under the bridge as it takes to work a normal job. I asked if he ever looked with envy at the construction workers, some of whom call out to him in a friendly way when they see him. They're out in the weather like he is, but then they get to go home. Home to families for most of them. Robert shook his head. The Bible says not to covet, he said.

The northbound lanes were due to open on Saturday, the day after I visited Robert. It will be a while longer before the southbound lanes open. "I need three weeks of good weather," Zuroweste said. "Who knows how long that will be?"

But if you happen to use the bridge, give a thought to Robert, who is down there below, acting almost like a night watchman, bothering nobody and coveting nothing.

A CHEESEBURGER WITH A SIDE OF JUSTICE

11.2.2008

On a Friday morning in August, Barry Brockman went to the Olivette Diner for breakfast. Brockman is 71, and more or less retired. He used to have an auto salvage and parts business, and now he works, but not too much, as a scrapper. He picks up junk metal and sells it for scrap. He goes out for breakfast two or three times a week. Until the day in question, the Olivette Diner was one of his haunts.

He ordered a cheeseburger on white toast. When the manager delivered the order, Brockman was unhappy with his sandwich. "The cheeseburger looked about the size of a silver dollar," he told me, and then he seemed to reconsider the description. "Maybe a little bigger than a silver dollar, but not by much." He continued his story. "I told Jack (the manager), 'I don't want this.' He told me, 'You're paying for it, anyway.'" Brockman said the owner of the diner was in that morning. "Look at this," Brockman said to the owner, pointing to what he thought was a diminutive cheeseburger. "If it was on a hamburger bun, it wouldn't look so small," is what the owner allegedly responded.

Brockman then ordered a grilled cheese sandwich. That sandwich was more to his liking. But when the bill came, the cheeseburger on white toast was on the bill. Brockman said he wasn't going to pay for it. He had words with the manager and left.

The next morning, Brockman returned to the diner. "You're not welcome here," said the manager. Brockman pulled a $5 bill out of his wallet. "I'm here to pay for the grilled cheese sandwich," he said. Then he slammed the $5 bill on the counter. Jeffery Gann, who was working the grill, nearly dropped his spatula. "I thought he was coming over the counter," Gann later told me. Then Brockman spoke to the manager. What he said is a matter of some dispute.

"I said, 'I ought to kick your (blank),'" Brockman told me.

The manager told police – and later me – that Brockman said, "I'm going to kick your (blanking blank)."

Forget the adjective. The law here is about the verbs. Should kick his blank? Or going to kick his blank? If he said he was going to do it, it's a threat, and that could classify as assault in the third degree. "A person commits the crime of assault in the third degree if the person purposely places another person in apprehension of immediate physical injury."

The manager called the police. Brockman left the diner but was pulled over as he drove east on Olive. "There were three police cars. I couldn't believe it," said Brockman. They took him to the police station. He wrote a statement. Concerning the alleged threat, he wrote, "I said I ought to kick your (blank)." He circled "ought."

Nevertheless, he was booked.

The case was supposed to go to trial last week in Olivette City Court, but Brockman hired a lawyer, Herbert Schaeffer, who got the charge amended to littering. "I think we worked out something that was quite reasonable," said Schaeffer.

Still, the case seemed intriguing. Brockman has had two heart attacks and has a defibrillator. He's a gruff-talking man, but was he really guilty of anything more serious than being a jerk?

I went to the diner for lunch Thursday. I ordered a cheeseburger. I did not order it on white toast as Brockman had suggested, but I believe a cheeseburger ought to be judged on a bun. In that sense, I agree with the owner. My cheeseburger was good. It cost $2.99. It was rather thin, but a good deal larger than a silver dollar. The man next to me also ordered a cheeseburger. I said to him, "What do you think of your cheeseburger?" He stared at me for a moment, and then said, "It's good."

Business was brisk at lunch, so I decided to return later to talk to the manager. By the way, he did not look like somebody who would feel threatened by Brockman. He had a beard. He was heavily tattooed. He wore an earring. He had a chain in his back pocket.

The manager said his name was Jack Jones. He said he was 49 years old. I asked him about the incident with Brockman, and he said, "I told him, 'You're not allowed in here. We don't want you in here,' and he said, 'I'm going to kick your (blanking blank).'"

I asked him if he thought Brockman was capable of doing that, and he said, "No. I didn't really think he could do it."

I asked the manager what he thought about the plea bargain. Was he all right with it?

"No, I think he should have gone to trial," he said. "How would you like it if somebody threatened you? It just goes to show that if you've got money, you can get away with anything."

He asked why the newspaper was interested in this. It's kind of a strange case, I said. "How do I know you're a reporter?" he asked. "Do you have a business card?" I looked in my wallet. I didn't have one. I showed him my reporter's notebook. It has the name of the newspaper on the front. "You can buy those anywhere," he said.

Later, I called the Olivette city prosecutor, Steven Fluhr. If the manager didn't feel apprehension, is it a valid charge? Fluhr said the case was prosecuted under city ordinances, and the language of the ordinance is such that a threat is enough for a charge. I told him the manager was unhappy with his decision to plea bargain the case.

"I decided in this instance that a plea bargain was appropriate. If somebody is unhappy with it, I'll gladly talk with him."

Brockman told me he has found new places to have breakfast.

Bill McClellan • Gently Down the Stream

'ANGEL' OF A REFUGEE IS TESTED BY HARD TIMES

12.20.2009

Miss Vickie arrived in St. Louis shortly after Hurricane Katrina devastated New Orleans. She was not from the city itself, but from Harvey, a small town on the western bank of the Mississippi River.

She was about 50 years old and a widow. She arrived here with two grown children, a son and a daughter. Her daughter had a small child. She found a place in north St. Louis.

"I hired her over the phone, sight unseen," said Mark Phillips, who owns Frontenac Cleaners on Clayton Road in Ladue. "Something about her just impressed me."

The first thing her new colleagues noticed was her size. She was a big woman, over 6 feet tall with a sturdy build.

"If you didn't know her, she could almost scare you," manager Donnie Dunn said. "But she was an angel. I mean that. If she touched your hand, you felt something."

She was an exemplary employee. She was an experienced presser. She didn't miss work. She arrived early and she worked cheerfully, but there was more to it.

"Miss Vickie was a mother," said co-worker Cornelia Reid. "Not only to her children but to others. She was a counselor and a healer. She always listened no matter what. She would cry with you. She would cry for you. She is an angel from God."

All this talk about angels. Was she, is she, religious?

"She didn't talk about it much, but when I'd go to her house, she'd always have gospel music playing," said Reid.

About a month and a half ago, people at work noticed a change. She seemed withdrawn. Something was wrong. Actually, a number of things were wrong. She was behind on her mortgage. Her house had been cited by a building inspector. Her 1986 Chrysler had quit running.

Last Friday, she went home and went to bed and stayed in bed all weekend. She did not get up to go to work on Monday. Her daughter called Dunn. "I don't know what I'm going to do with my mama," she said. Bring her in tomorrow, Dunn said.

Phillips had decided to intervene. He talked to her Tuesday morning. "You've been a great employee. We're not going to let you lose your house," he said. He also called the city building inspector whose name was on the citations. The inspector told him that none of the citations were serious and no immediate action was planned. "I told her that," Phillips said, "but the face I was looking at – she wasn't there."

Shortly after noon that day, Dunn noticed she wasn't at her station. Somebody told him Miss Vickie had gone out. Dunn went to the window and looked out. He saw her walking into the Heartland Bank across the street.

"I figured she was going in for a loan," he said.

Moments later, Reid looked out and saw Miss Vickie coming from behind the fire station next to the bank. She then started to walk along Clayton Road. Reid called Dunn and the two of them went out to talk to her. She was carrying her coat. I'm walking home, said Miss Vickie. You can't walk all the way to north St. Louis, Dunn said. He went back to the cleaners and got his truck.

The three of them drove to Miss Vickie's house in the 2600 block of Belt Avenue without much talking. Dunn figured she had not gotten the loan and was depressed. He said something about wanting to help if there was anything he could do. Miss Vickie said, "I was under a lot of stress, but I'm fine now. I've taken care of my family. I robbed that bank."

She opened her coat. There was more cash than Dunn had ever seen. More than $5,000. Miss Vickie said that she had given the teller a note in which she claimed to have a gun. "Oh my God, Miss Vickie!" screamed Reid.

Dunn decided they had to get back to Ladue immediately and return the money. "I thought maybe I could explain this to somebody. We do the uniforms for the Ladue police department. I know a lot of the police."

He was on St. Charles Rock Road heading west when he heard the helicopter. He was at a stoplight when the police blocked the road. There had been a tracking device with the money.

The three of them were pulled out of the car and arrested. Eventually, things were sorted out, and Dunn and Reid were released. Miss Vickie was charged with first-degree robbery. Bail was set at $100,000.

I talked with Miss Vickie's daughter Friday. She works at a Home Depot. She said they were not in immediate danger of losing the house, but apparently there had been some threatening letters and her mother was convinced they would lose the house at the end of the month. Same sort of thing with the citations. There was nothing like this in Harvey, the daughter said.

I stopped by the jail. Herb Bernsen, director of the county Department of Justice Services, said that he could not disclose any specifics but that Victoria Edwards had been seen by mental health professionals almost as soon as she arrived Tuesday. She is currently being held in the infirmary. She declined to speak with me.

Back at the cleaners, Phillips had an idea. "Guilty by admission, released by compassion," he said.

FOSTER CHILD MAKES GOOD; MOTHER OF 3 ADOPTS 3 MORE

4.16.2007

Shortly before noon on Sunday, six kids came tumbling out of a well-kept town house on Penrose Avenue on the city's north side. They were headed to a nearby park. They had a reprieve from church because the family car is on the fritz. Who knows what's wrong? Old age, maybe. At 15, the car is older than any of the kids, who are 14, 13, 12, 10, 7 and 2.

The head of the family is Gina Mattison. She's 31. Life is hectic when you're a single mother with six kids, but she's not complaining. She asked for this life. Literally. She adopted three of the kids. They were her sister's kids, and they were about to go into foster care.

That's a lifestyle Gina remembers too well.

She was 5 when the state took her away from her own mother. It's all a little fuzzy. She was one of five kids. She lived in Springfield, Ill. Her father was abusive to her mother. Her mother took the kids to California, but her mom had problems of her own, and the state soon took the kids and put them into the foster care system.

Gina stayed in the system for a few years. How many families? She can't remember. She tries to think of the names. She rattles off a few and then shakes her head. Some of them were very nice, she said. Most of the time she was separated from her siblings. Occasionally, she was with a brother.

When Gina was 12, she was sent to Springfield to be with her father, but that didn't work, and she wound up with her grandmother. Two sisters were with her, and that was too much for her grandmother. The kids were put back in the foster care system. There were more bad times than good. When Gina was 17, she ran away from a group home and went to Las Vegas with a boyfriend. She got a housekeeping job in a hotel.

She and her boyfriend returned to Springfield after two years, and Gina went back to high school and graduated. She was still with her boyfriend, and she got pregnant.

They moved to St. Louis and Gina attended a medical assistants school. It was a nine-month program. She graduated and began working for St. Louis University. She had borrowed $3,000 to attend the school. About the time she graduated, her boyfriend moved back to Las Vegas.

She later took out another student loan and got an associate's degree in computer programming from Sanford-Brown College. She also got in another relationship and had another child. She got another job with another hospital and she had another baby. Then she broke up with the father, and there she was – a 29-year-old single mother of three. But she had some education and some drive. She was living in the county in a two-bedroom house. Life looked rather promising.

For kids who've grown up in turmoil, that's a success story. More common, perhaps, is what befell one of Gina's sisters. Substance abuse problems, abusive relationships and then state intervention. In this instance, the state declared that Gina's sister was incapable of protecting her children from harm, particularly from abusive boyfriends.

The sister moved to Georgia but applied for public assistance and was caught. The children were going to be put in foster care.

Gina stepped in. She was given temporary custody last June and then decided to adopt them. The kids needed stability. She did not want them to drift as she had. The state told her she'd need a larger place so she had to give up that house in the county. She applied for Section 8 and got the place on Penrose. It's a rough neighborhood, and it's right up against Interstate 70, but so what?

The adoption was finalized in February. At first, the transition was rocky. Her nieces and nephew started out poorly in school. Now they're doing much better. Gina is back in school, too. She is attending St. Louis Community College at Forest Park. She plans on becoming a nurse. She helps the kids with their homework, and then when they go to bed, she does her own.

When I stopped by Sunday morning, all the kids were in the living room. Everybody was polite and well-behaved, but it was clear they were eager to get out and enjoy the day. Eventually, Gina released them. I asked her how she was doing.

"We don't have the finest things," she said, and she laughed. "But we've got love. It's getting done, thank God."

WHEN A STORM OF WORDS GOES TO COURT, DELAY CAN BE KIND

12.03.2006

Norman Sussman was supposed to be in court at 9 a.m. Thursday, but the forecast called for snow, and when I spoke to him the night before, he assured me that he would not be venturing out into bad weather just to stand in front of a judge who had already been paid off and so on and so forth.

Sussman is himself a storm, a hurricane of words. Phone conversations generally end with the other party saying, "Norman, I'm going to hang up now," and Sussman continuing to talk nonstop until the realization finally comes that the line is dead.

I stopped by his place Thursday morning a little after 8 to see if he had changed his mind about going to court. A cold rain was falling.

He lives in an apartment one block north of the Delmar Loop. Stuff is piled everywhere. Much of it is in boxes. Although a visitor might think that Sussman has not yet unpacked, he has lived in the apartment for 15 years and six months. He moved in shortly after his mother died. He is 58 years old. He has long white hair and an unkempt white beard.

"Yes, I'm going to court," he said. He said that his caseworker had insisted he go, and that she would be arriving any minute to take him.

He launched into a spirited discussion of his case. "There is no need for them to evict me. They have plenty of other buildings. They can't evict me, can they? Do you think they can just take my stuff and put it out on the street? Do you know what they told me? They said they have million-dollar lawyers who've appeared in front of the Supreme Court ..."

The "they" in this case are the people at Washington University. The university's Quadrangle Housing owns the apartment building. Sussman's dispute with Quadrangle Housing has to do with his rent.

Sussman used to receive something called a mental health rental subsidy, but that was canceled when he was approved for a Section 8 voucher, and so the money from the subsidy that was automatically going to Quadrangle Housing was cut off. That subsidy had covered about half of his $400-a-month rent. He had continued to pay his share but had fallen into arrears.

Why hadn't the Section 8 voucher made up the difference? Because he was not living in Section 8 housing. Adding to the confusion was a letter he showed me from Quadrangle stating he was not in arrears.

With any sort of luck, everything would be explained in court. The lawyer from the university would give the university's side, and then Sussman – or maybe his caseworker – would give his side.

I studied some paperwork while we waited for his caseworker. Sussman receives $519 each month in Social Security benefits, and $104 from Supplemental Security Income. His bank statement showed a balance of zero.

His caseworker arrived. Her name is Kathy Carmody, and she works for Places for People, an organization that helps people with mental disorders.

Division 42 had the Docket of Despair on Thursday morning. Finance companies versus people. As Carmody and Sussman approached the door, Carmody pointed to the sign that read, "Quiet Please. Court in Session."

Sussman nodded and kept talking. Inside, the bailiff read names aloud, and if no one responded from the gallery, one of the lawyers at a table would say to the judge, "Default!"

Senior Judge Ellis Gregory was presiding, and I thought that boded well for Sussman. The law is the law, of course, but I doubted that Gregory would interpret it in such a way that a fellow like Sussman would be tossed into the street in the freezing rain during the holiday season. When it came time to figure out what to do, Sussman and Carmody were called to the lawyers' table to confer with Richard Abrams, the lawyer for Washington University.

Sussman started talking up a storm. Carmody tried to get a word in. Abrams tried to get a word in. I heard snatches of conversation.

"Nobody wants you to be homeless." "Well, I will be." "I had no idea." "My father was married six times."

After a few minutes, a decision had been reached.

Everything was put off until Jan. 11.

Later, I spoke to Carmody. She said that she was going to try to find Sussman another apartment in the same neighborhood. Maybe she'd try to get him back on the mental health rental subsidy.

At least there was time to try to work things out. Best of all, Sussman will be at home for the holidays.

ECCENTRIC LIVES, 'ART' ARE SIBLINGS' LEGACY

7.15.2009

On the day after Christmas 2006, a St. Louis County EMS crew responded to a 911 call from a house in the upper-middle-class suburb of Olivette.

They found 91-year-old Betty Wynn lying in the dining room. She was surrounded by mounds of trash. Also in the house was the man who had made the call – Betty's 85-year-old brother, Sam Lachterman. He looked like an elderly Robinson Crusoe. He was dressed in tattered clothes. His long hair and beard were wildly unkempt.

The EMS crew put Betty on a stretcher and rushed her to St. John's Mercy Medical Center, where she was declared dead. Sam came along in the ambulance. A social worker told him he would not be allowed to return to the house. From what the EMS crew had said, the house would almost certainly be condemned. The social worker asked Sam for the name of a friend, somebody to call in this hour of need.

After a long moment's thought, he came up with a name – Pat Zollner. She was more Betty's friend than Sam's, but that was to be expected. Betty was the one who interacted with the outside world. When Olivette officials tried to force Betty and Sam to remove a dead tree in their backyard, Betty was the one who went to court to fight the city. She argued that the dead tree was a piece of art. The judge asked a Washington University art professor for help. The professor turned the matter over to his students. If the role of art is to get people talking about society's values, the dead tree is obviously art, one student said. Olivette dropped the case.

Zollner had met Betty years earlier. Zollner was working as a secretary at Washington University. Betty and Sam haunted the campus. Really, they were like ghostly spirits. They went to lectures and concerts, mostly ones at which food was served.

For a while, they lived in a car that they parked on a university parking lot. That got them banned from the campus, but the ban was lifted when sympathetic faculty intervened and argued that the brother and sister, both graduates of the university, were part of the fabric of the place.

About a month after Betty's death, a standing-room-only crowd of about 120 faculty and staff members gathered in a second-story lounge at Washington University to remember Betty, a 1936 graduate of the School of Social Work. She was remembered not for her work – she worked only briefly – but for the strange path she chose in life. Sam was at that gathering.

I saw him again some months later. I was speaking at the University of Missouri-St. Louis. My topic was something like, "St. Louis Characters." Sam was sitting in the back of the room. By then, he looked less like Robinson Crusoe and more like Albert Einstein. His clothes were clean, but his white hair was still wild. Besides, while he might have been Robinson Crusoe in a certain sense – marooned on an island of his own making – he was closer to Einstein. He had a Ph.D. in math from Washington University, and he had been a math professor at St. Louis University from 1964 to 1974. Former students have told me he was a strange duck even then – not mean, but impatient with students who didn't grasp mathematics as easily as he did. He quit in 1974. By the way, even when he was a professor, he lived with his sister. He never married. She had been married once, long ago and briefly.

Last week I got a call from Zollner. Sam died, she told me. She was at his house in Olivette. I drove over.

The first thing I noticed was how normal the place looked. Back when Betty was alive, the place was always something of a wreck, even from the outside. They had inherited the house from a brother. Or bought it from a brother. I was never sure.

Betty and Sam were unlikely suburbanites, and the house showed it. But after Betty died, Zollner and some friends cleaned it up and got everything up to code. Sam, who had been staying at Zollner's house, moved back in. Now, it looked normal. Inside, too. Nothing fancy, but it was clean. That seemed remarkable. Sam was a pack rat. He had thousands of records. Classical music. He got most of them for nothing. When libraries began throwing them out, Sam scooped them up.

Did he ever listen to them? No, said Zollner. His turntable was broken. Somebody got him a new one, but he was too stubborn to use it. He intended to fix his, and that was that.

Zollner told me that toward the end, Sam admitted to some regrets. Long ago, he had a girlfriend. Maybe he should have married her and lived a more traditional life. Her name was Suzanne. I thought of the Leonard Cohen song – "She is wearing rags and feathers from Salvation Army counters" – which I have always associated with Betty, who was, regrets aside, Sam's lifelong partner on a very odd journey.

As I left, I glanced into the backyard. The dead tree remains.

WAR ON DRUGS IS A HARD SELL WHEN JUSTICE IS A CASUALTY

3.5.2008

Last week The Associated Press reported that for the first time in our nation's history, more than one of every 100 adults is in jail or prison.

"Whether per capita or in raw numbers, it's more than any other nation," the story said. This week this newspaper reported that hundreds of thousands of fugitives successfully avoid arrest merely by moving from one state to another. This group includes rapists, child molesters and even cop killers. The criminal justice system is simply overwhelmed.

Have we, as a people, really become so bad that our prisons, numerous as they are, cannot hold all of our criminals? How come the presidential candidates aren't talking about this?

Let me tell you about Lougene Thomas. He was in federal court last week. He was charged with possession with intent to distribute crack cocaine, being a felon in possession of a firearm and possession of a firearm during a drug offense.

He was arrested in March of last year in front of an apartment building on Chippewa Street in St. Louis. Police had received information that a person was selling drugs at that location. Two marked cars drove over to check it out. Sure enough, there was Thomas, in plain view, handing somebody something and being handed something in return. The officers stopped and got out of their cars. The fellow who had made the exchange with Thomas took off running and got away. Thomas was not so fortunate. He started walking back to the building and while doing so, threw a baggie down. The baggie contained crack.

Thomas agreed to let the police search his apartment and directed them to the closet where he had more crack in a shoebox. Also, a pistol was in the shoebox. In total, he had about nine grams of crack.

He was on parole for a drug offense. In fact, that's probably why he was selling in front of his apartment. He was wearing a monitor. He had to stay close to home.

He was charged in federal court, and the system began to grind along. Thomas had no money and was appointed a federal public defender. Although the case was essentially hopeless, the federal public defender diligently prepared a defense. He hired a document examiner from Illinois as an expert witness to determine whether the signature on the consent to search form was that of Thomas. By this time, Thomas was denying that he had authorized the search. At an evidentiary hearing in September, the expert witness said he could not be sure about the signature.

Thomas also testified at the hearing. He said that a frog – "an animal frog," he called it – had been hopping around in the grass just before the police arrived. Perhaps that is what the officers had seen him handing to the fellow who ran.

This "frog defense" was intriguing enough that I went to court last week when Thomas was scheduled to go to trial. But instead of going with his defense, he pleaded guilty. He'll be sentenced later. He'll probably get 10 years. That's a lot of time, but he was looking at 20 years if he went to trial and lost.

At any rate, that's who we're putting in prison. Guys like Lougene Thomas. He's an addict. He certainly wasn't making a lot of money. He was probably selling enough so he could use for free. Even though he wasn't hard to catch, we spent a good deal of money on his case. At least three different assistant U.S. attorneys worked on the case. After Thomas had a falling out with his federal public defender, the court appointed him a private attorney. We paid for him. We paid for the document examiner. Now we're going to pay for 10 years of incarceration.

What if we legalized drugs? What if we decided that this prohibition stuff isn't working for drugs any more than it worked for booze? The police can chase the street dealers from one corner to another. They can even arrest the dealers, but they are quickly replaced. That's true for the low-level guys like Thomas, or the kingpins like Pablo Escobar. As long as there is a demand, there will be a supply. We can't stop people from using drugs. Lord knows we've tried.

If we took a fraction of the money we spend on catching the druggies and prosecuting and incarcerating them and spent it on drug education and treatment programs, we would be so much better off. Instead, we fill up our prisons and overwhelm the criminal justice system to the point that the real bad guys can get away.

The politicians won't talk about it because it's just too risky to admit that the emperor has no clothes. It's so much safer to muddle along.

WEE FOLK CAN'T SPIN MAGIC
LIKE THAT OF DAD AND DAUGHTER

10.1.2006

Sydney Barnason is 10 years old. She attends the Academy of the Sacred Heart in St. Charles, and she is active in sports. She plays soccer, basketball and softball, and she swims. But before she got started in sports, she wasn't so active. She liked to watch television, and one beautiful Saturday morning a couple of years ago, she had just settled in for a cartoon marathon when her father, Jim, suggested they go for a hike.

No thanks, she said.

But her father was not easily deterred. That should come as no surprise. When Sydney had balked at eating vegetables, her mother, Melissa, had said sternly, "Just eat them!" But Jim took cauliflower and broccoli and put them in a blender, and he threw in some fruit and some juice, and he made smoothies. So on this Saturday morning, he did not order his daughter to go on a hike. Instead, he told her she was ready to learn about leprechaun hunting.

Sydney knew that her dad had grown up in Nebraska and had been a hunter since boyhood. What's more, the family dog, Herb, was a black lab, a hunting dog. Mostly, her dad and Herb hunted pheasants. But leprechauns?

It's a rather long story, her dad explained. Fortunately, he was a fine storyteller. Melissa grew up in St. Louis, and has siblings here, and that means that Sydney has cousins, and some of the cousins closest to her – Mary Kate and Dan McGraugh and Alexander Horner, for instance – would tell you that Uncle Jim was better than television. In his stories, kids themselves were characters.

So Jim explained a bit about leprechaun hunting to his daughter. First of all, it's a child's sport. You have to catch a leprechaun by the time you're 10. After that, it's too late. But once you catch one, he or she is your friend forever. They're magical creatures, of course, so it's good to have one as a friend. For instance, a leprechaun will grant you three wishes, but you have to wait until you're 25 to have the wishes granted. You catch a leprechaun by finding at least three articles belonging to the creature. A gold ring is a must. A piece of clothing counts. A hat, or a buckle or bell from a shoe. Stuff like that.

Jim happened to know all this because he had caught a leprechaun in Nebraska. That leprechaun, whose name was Lucky, had followed Jim to St. Louis and now lived in Queeny Park.

And that is where Jim and Sydney and Herb went to look for leprechauns. They didn't have much luck that first day. Herb caught the scent of a leprechaun on one or two occasions, but that was about it.

They began to go hunting more regularly. Their luck began to turn. They found a hat. Then they found some felt from a leprechaun jacket. They found some corn and biscuits one day, and then they found tennis balls with leprechaun names written on them. (All leprechaun names begin with L.) Herb often bounded around, clearly on the scent. One time, Sydney felt someone tap on her shoulder. She whirled to her father. "Was that you?" "Was what me?" There was magic going on in the woods.

For her eighth birthday, Sydney asked for a metal detector. That might help with the ring and shoe buckles.

It did. Sydney found a ring. She had caught a leprechaun. What now? "You exchange letters and begin your friendship," explained Jim.

Sydney had a lot of questions for her leprechaun. There was so much that she didn't understand. For instance, you have to be 40 years old or have a child of your own before you can see a leprechaun. Why is that? And salt freezes a leprechaun. Why?

So Sydney and her leprechaun began exchanging letters. There was a place in the woods where they'd leave each other letters. Because Sydney's leprechaun was a little girl – only 100 years old – there were certain things she couldn't explain. But she was able to talk about herself a bit. Her name was Lucy, and her father's name was Lucky, and her mother's name was Louise. They were from Nebraska, where her father had been caught by a little boy many years ago. Lucy didn't know the little boy's name, but her dad had granted him three wishes – a great dog, a beautiful wife and a beautiful and healthy daughter.

What a small and magical world it is!

The letters went on for a while, and so did the leprechaun hunting at Queeny Park. Cousin Mary Kate caught one. Her name was Lowenfle. They exchanged letters, too.

Gradually, though, life came between the children and the leprechauns. Sydney became involved in sports. Saturday mornings were spent on the soccer field. Or in the pool or on the basketball court. This past February, Jim was taking his daughter to a basketball game. She asked, "Daddy, are leprechauns real?"

Yes, he said.

A few days later, Melissa and Jim were taking Sydney to an indoor soccer game. She asked them about Santa Claus.

The spirit of Christmas is real, they said. But is Santa himself a real character? No. And the tooth fairy and the Easter bunny? No and no. Are leprechauns real? No.

Sydney was furious. The hoax had been so elaborate. She felt so, well, betrayed. Jim was crushed that she felt that way. But they were very close, and before long, they were all right again.

Jim died in July. He died suddenly while bicycle riding. He was 46. Melissa said she did not yet have a death certificate, but she figures it was a heart attack.

Sydney will be 11 in November. She does not yet know where she'll go to high school, and she has no idea what she'll do when she grows up. But she is sure of one thing. When she has children of her own, she will take them leprechaun hunting.

SOCIAL GAFFE IS REALLY
AN ACT OF KINDNESS IN DISGUISE

11.26.2007

I dropped a glass Friday night. It happened at a cocktail party. Yes, a cocktail party. That's an important fact. This was not a bunch of people getting together with drinking being more or less incidental to the occasion. Drinking was central to this occasion. The invitation said, You are invited to a cocktail party.

To put the whole thing into some context, it was the night after Thanksgiving. My daughter was home from California. She teaches high school biology. My son was home from the University of Wisconsin.

My son was recently sued by the music industry. He was one of a number of students in the Wisconsin system who were accused of downloading music. He called to tell me about the lawsuit and to inform me that he knew a good lawyer in Madison. "How do you know a good lawyer in Madison?" I asked. "What do you have, somebody on retainer?" It turned out that a friend of his had gotten a ticket for underage drinking and the lawyer had done a nice job with the ticket. Yes, but this was a different and perhaps more serious issue. I said I'd have an attorney in St. Louis handle the lawsuit. I did. The attorney looked into the matter and explained that the music industry has been filing these lawsuits in an effort to frighten people away from downloading music. A woman in Minnesota went to court and lost $120,000. That frightened me. I decided to accept the settlement offer. We had to pay the music industry $4,000.

I do not even know what downloading is. I was reminded of a time several years ago when water began seeping up through a drain into my basement. A sewer line was ruptured. A man from the sewer district came to my house and said that if the break was under my property, I would have to pay, but if the break was at the "main line," the sewer district would pay. He showed me some red crystals and said he was going to do something with the crystals and then he

was going to look at a manhole down the street and if the water was red, the sewer district would pay. Maybe it was the other way around. If it was red, I'd have to pay. I went with him to the manhole, and sure enough, whichever way meant that I would have to pay was the way it was. That cost me $7,000.

So I am not a stranger to unexpected and mysterious expenses.

Of course, my son felt guilty. He knows that $4,000 is a lot of money.

Perhaps I should have given him a lecture about responsibility when he came home for the holiday, but that is not my style. Instead, I avoided the subject of responsibility at Thanksgiving dinner and talked about more pleasant things. The next night I went to the cocktail party.

I would not say I am clumsy as much as I am awkward. I am the sort of person who would have been voted "Most Likely to Drop a Glass" in high school. It's just something I would do. If there were an etiquette boot camp and the drill instructor were to line us all up and say, "Look at the man on your left. Go ahead, look at him! Now look at the man on your right! In six months, one of you will drop a glass!" all three of us would figure it would be me.

I should also explain that this cocktail party was in honor of two young people who are engaged. So there were a number of young people at the party, and a number of people like myself. Mature people, so to speak. And toward the end of the party, I dropped a glass.

Here is something you would learn in etiquette boot camp: If you are going to drop a glass, do it early in the evening. If you do it late in the evening, some people will presume that your coordination is at issue.

I believe some of the young people at the party made that presumption about me. One of the young people at the party knows my son, and immediately sent him a text message. "Ur Pa drppd gls." Or something to that effect. Another young person ran into my daughter at a different party later that night and told her.

For the rest of the weekend, who was treated like the irresponsible person? Was it the young man who downloaded music? No.

So I feel bad about dropping that glass, but in a sense, it was a random act of kindness.

THE VOICE ON THE OTHER END OF THE LINE HAS A REAL LIFE, AND FEELINGS, TOO

8.20.2006

You're in the middle of dinner and the phone rings. You leave the table and answer the phone. "Hello," you say.

"My name is Ellen. I'm from Premiere Equity. How are you today? I'm calling to offer you a free quote on your mortgage..."

Ellen Kahan does not have a mortgage herself. She lives in an apartment in University City. She is 59 years old. She works at the call center from 5 p.m. to 9 p.m. Monday through Thursday and from 9 a.m. to 1 p.m. on Saturday. She does not have a car and so she takes the bus. When she started her job a couple of years ago, the bus trips were an ordeal, but eventually she mastered the task and now it's easy.

Of course, life never stays easy for long. The bus routes are changing and come the last week of this month, Ellen is going to have to take two buses to get to work. She'll have to transfer. She is not looking forward to this, but she is sure she can handle it.

She was raised in University City. When she learned to walk, it was not with a normal gait. A doctor suggested braces to pull her heel cord down. The braces were regularly tightened. The pain was fierce. It is among her earliest memories. When she was seven, she had surgery.

Those were difficult days. Some children made fun of her because of her limp. Also, she had dyslexia, but that diagnosis was not in vogue in those days, and so she was classified as marginally retarded. She had to repeat third grade. She used to hate school. Getting out of bed was a chore. She did not want to go to school. Mostly, she hated being who she was.

She had an older sister who was very bright. Her sister went to Brandeis University, and then to Washington University, and then to Stanford. She became an English professor and moved to the East Coast.

Ellen did not complete University City High School. She just couldn't handle it. She spent her senior year at a place called University Academy. It is no longer in operation.

After high school, she went to work for her father. He ran a film distribution business. Ellen liked working for her father, but that did not mean that life was always easy. She was hospitalized for depression. Later, she did clerical work in a doctor's office, but she eventually lost that job because she was taking her personal problems to work. She said she was not surprised when she was fired. She had heard talk, she said.

In 1995, she went on disability for her depression. She receives about $1,100 a month. Still, she did not – and does not – want to just sit around. So she got the job as a telemarketer.

I visited her at her apartment earlier this week. She talked about her lifestyle. It is a simple one. She has a television, but not a computer. She eats mostly frozen dinners. That greatly reduces the need to cook or to clean up. In fact, she has a housekeeper come in once a month.

She said she once had a new car. That was when she worked at the doctor's office. But she didn't like driving. It was always stressful, and she got rid of her last car in 1998. She said she had never had a serious boyfriend, but she did see a man for a while. She also said she once had a toy poodle, but she gave it to the doorman at the apartment where she was living.

I asked about her job. When you interrupt somebody's dinner – and when you work 5 to 9, you do a lot of that – how do most people respond? And do you get accustomed to the angry responses to the point that they don't hurt?

She said people often just hang up once they realize she's a telemarketer. Sometimes they're mean. "Some are very caustic," she said. But others are nice. They say, "No, thank you." Ellen said she appreciates that.

She recently sent me a letter, which is why I visited her. She had ended the letter by quoting Robert Frost – "Miles to go before I sleep, and miles to go before I sleep." That's a great attitude to have, I said, and she laughed. "Sometimes I wonder if it's true," she said.

So now you know a little bit about the person behind the voice that might just interrupt your dinner.

BLACK CAT WINDS UP COSTING A LOT OF GREEN

2.15.2010

Sometime late this summer, a black cat showed up at a subdivision in Shiloh. It was not a wild animal. It had a collar and a tag with a phone number on it. It would sometimes saunter onto the deck of Rick Humphrey's house and look in through the French doors.

Humphrey would sometimes go out and pet the cat. He never fed it.

Still, he began to develop a relationship with the cat, at least as much of a relationship as a person can develop with a cat, especially a cat that occasionally shows up on the person's deck.

But here is something to know about Humphrey. He is 56 years old. He is married with no children. Many years ago, when he was young and single and living in his first apartment, the couple who lived in the apartment next to his had a cat. It was a great cat. If you whistled, it would come to you and let you pet it. He really liked that cat. Once or twice, the couple asked if he wanted the cat. He said no. One day, the couple took the cat to the shelter. Humphrey thought about going to the shelter and claiming the cat. He did not. His failure to do so still gnaws at him.

One day this fall, he called the number on the black cat's tag. No answer. Later, a neighbor told Humphrey he had called the number and gotten an answer, but the person had not come to get the cat.

Sometime later, the cat showed up again but without the collar.

When the weather started to turn bad in December, Humphrey put a box on the deck for the cat to sleep in. Also, he put out some food. The cat spent a couple of nights in the box, and ate the food, but the third morning, it was gone. That happened to be a wintry, gusty morning, and Humphrey was disappointed to see the cat gone, but he headed to work. He is a financial analyst at Boeing.

His wife, Eileen, who does hospice social work, called him. The cat was back and yowling at the French doors. She could not leave it out in this weather. She was going to let it in the garage. Also, she was going to make an appointment with a veterinarian for that afternoon.

By the way, Rick had been calling the cat Aretha, as in Aretha Franklin. Black and cool.

The first thing the vet informed Eileen was that the cat was a male. So Aretha became Rhett, as in Rhett Butler. Cool and suave.

Although Rhett had been neutered at some point – somebody had spent some money on him – the vet was starting from scratch, as far as shots go. Who knew what Rhett was due? So he got them all.

He tested positive for feline leukemia. That's actually a virus. Treatment is not cheap, but the Humphreys had made a commitment to this cat. So Rhett was treated for feline leukemia.

Then he developed a stomach problem. Fortunately, that too was treatable.

By the time the stomach problem was treated, the Humphreys had spent a total of more than $600 on the cat.

Two weeks ago, the Humphreys came home from work and found Rhett wobbling around in the kitchen. Eileen took him to the vet the next day. He was anemic. A series of tests would be required to get to the cause. The tests would be about $400. Also, he would need a blood transfusion. That could be done at an emergency clinic in Collinsville that has donor cats on call. The transfusion itself would be about $350, but depending on what the tests show, the total costs could fall between $700 and $1,000.

We'll do it, said the Humphreys.

The tests showed that during his life outside, Rhett had picked up four different flea- and tick-borne pathogens that had attached themselves to his red blood cells and his antibodies were attacking his red blood cells. That had brought on the anemia.

Three weeks of antibiotics and steroids could fix that.

We did not let this cat into our house just to die, said Rick.

As the Humphreys began administering this treatment, which is not inexpensive, I happened to write a column about a bird-feeder in my backyard. I wrote that my cat and I enjoy watching the birds. I mentioned that I bought my cat at Soulard Farmers Market in 1992. I wrote that I paid six bucks for the cat. I wrote: "It went against everything I believed in to pay for a cat – 'In

America, cats are free,' I told the children – but they were in love with the kitten in the cage."

Humphrey read that column and he sent me a note. He was polite, but firm. He thought I had given my children some faulty information. "There is no such thing as a free cat," he wrote.

SALOON OWNER'S GLORY DAYS WENT UP IN FLAMES

5.9.2007

Many years ago, there was a saloon in Kirksville, Mo., called Too Tall Tucks. It burned down 24 years ago and was rebuilt as Too Tall Two Spirits and Eatery.

In March of 2003, the Truman State University newspaper gave Too Tall Two the "Best Bar in Town" award. The next month, the owner of the saloon, Debbie Masten, was elected to the Kirksville City Council. She was then selected by her fellow council members as mayor.

But the good times did not last. Or perhaps those good times were never really so good. In the early morning hours of Jan. 1, 2005, there was another fire. Investigators said it had been deliberately set. Masten was eventually arrested and charged with arson.

Her trial began in federal court Tuesday.

Assistant U.S. Attorney Dean Hoag is a veteran prosecutor. He could be called Too Intense but not Too Tall. He is stocky. He glares at people. He paces back and forth with his arms folded across his chest.

In his opening statement, Hoag told the jurors that Too Tall Two was a money-loser. He said that in the last two months of '04, the saloon management had bounced 122 checks. He said that Masten was in trouble with the IRS for failure to pay withholding taxes. He told the jurors that arson investigators would testify that the fire had started in two batches of paper, and that three of Masten's employees would testify that those batches of paper had not been there when they left the saloon and that they had been the last to leave except for Masten.

Circumstantial evidence to be sure, but it sounded pretty strong.

To me, anyway. Probably not to most of the crowd. Most of the spectators were on Masten's side – friends and family. Although the public pays for insurance fraud through higher premiums, nobody shows up at court to see that justice is done for an insurance company. In addition to Masten's supporters, a television reporter from Kirksville was in attendance.

If Hoag's recitation of the facts painted a picture of a failing business and a desperate owner, defense attorney Douglas Forsyth saw things a bit differently. Yes, the business had been sliding in the final months of '04, but that was only because Masten and her husband were both dealing with dying parents. And financially strapped? Hardly. They had an excavation company, a car wash and money in the bank, Forsyth said.

He also suggested that his client was an honorable woman, a fighter and was not afraid to make enemies. She had been the volleyball coach at Truman State and had then sued the university over gender inequality. As mayor, she had taken on the fire department over excessive overtime. Forsyth also mentioned that Masten was a Democrat.

Perhaps those things would give the jury something to think about. Enemies everywhere.

But what about the fire? Forsyth suggested a karaoke machine. It had caused some kind of electrical problem, he said.

In voir dire, when the attorneys were selecting the jury, Forsyth had asked the potential jurors about their knowledge of electricity. As I listened to his opening statement, I wondered, had he wanted people with knowledge of electricity on the jury, or had he wanted to keep them off the jury?

I also wondered about Masten. Had she been a popular mayor? I called the office of the Kirksville Daily Express and talked to editor Greg Orear.

In the beginning, she was popular, he said. As is true in a lot of university towns, there is a town-gown split in Kirksville, and despite her background with the university, Masten was seen as a town person, Orear said. She was going to bring a business sense to government.

In a controversial move, she sold some town land and she did not take criticism well, Orear said. She was confrontational. She alienated people.

Then came the fire. Almost immediately, she was suspected. She resigned and left town.

Looking back, the heady days of '03 must seem like a long time ago. She was a popular mayor. She had a seemingly successful business. The school paper said it was the Best Bar in Town. Now, I wonder if she wishes that the first fire had been the last and that Too Tall Tucks had never been rebuilt.

DID FANTASY, RUM AND COKE SPARK FIRE AT SALOON?

5.16.2007

The arson trial of Debbie Masten, former mayor of Kirksville, left "Law and Order" and veered toward "American Idol" on Tuesday when the defense played a videotape of a karaoke singer.

I have always admired karaoke singers. They put their fantasy lives on the line in front of strangers. Most of us keep our fantasy lives strictly to ourselves.

For all you know, the guy in the next cubicle dreams that he is a secret agent. Or maybe a baseball player, a homicide detective or an international diamond thief.

Now and then, somebody will lose control and confuse his fantasy life with his real one. That is almost always disastrous. Last month, Michael Weilbacher was fined $3,000 and put on two years of probation for wearing military medals he had not been awarded. Although he had never been in the service, he joined a Marine Corps League detachment and went to a dance wearing a Navy Cross, a Silver Star and two Bronze Stars. That sort of hardware is going to raise suspicions even if it's not on the chest of an overweight guy who is too young to have been in Vietnam and too old for Iraq. How could he have expected to get away with such a clumsy deception? How clouded his mind must have been, how blurry the line between fantasy and reality.

Only the karaoke singers dare to be open. You can see their dreams. That fellow is Tom Jones. That one is David Clayton Powell. And look, there's Mama Cass. They are willing to go public with their fantasies. I am not talking about the folks who have a couple of drinks, get talked into a song and then perform in a self-conscious, half-hearted way. I'm talking about the serious karaoke singers, the ones who can tell you which bars have karaoke on what nights.

The videotape shown in court Tuesday was taken by the mother of the singer. On the witness stand, under oath, the mother described her daughter as a "vocal artist."

It was an apt description, I'm sure. The audio quality of the tape was not so hot, but the singer wailed away with a seriousness of purpose that left no doubt of her artistry. She moved her head, she waved her arms. She could have been the main act at Riverport. Who was she being? I am not hip enough to know this latest generation of singers, but she was somebody good, I can tell you that. Somebody country.

The videotape was a key element for the defense in the trial. Masten is accused of torching her Kirksville saloon in the early hours of Jan. 1, 2005. Defense attorney Douglas Forsyth contends that the fire began in the wiring and that problems with the karaoke machine were indicative of deeper electrical problems. The videotape showed that certain lights went on and off. Furthermore, there was a problem with the speakers.

Several witnesses then testified that, yes, they had seen the lights flashing or had heard popping sounds.

These witnesses were friends of Masten, and they testified that they came to her saloon, Too Tall Two, every New Year's Eve. They even sat at the same table every year.

They seemed nice. They seemed fun. One said that she had participated in the karaoke that night, and I was disappointed that Assistant U.S. Attorney Dean Hoag did not ask her what song she had sung.

Instead, he asked about drinking. How much did they drink? A good bit, most of them said. Beer and Jell-O shots were mentioned. Hoag wanted to know about Masten. Did she drink with them during the evening? Yes, she did.

By the way, she was drinking rum and coke.

To me, that speaks to a certain fantasy life. When I think of rum, I think of islands, trade winds, beaches and sunshine. That's a long way from a winter's night in Kirksville, Mo.

With his questions about Masten's drinking, I wondered if Hoag was trying to suggest that the alleged arson was a spur-of-the-moment thing, not really planned out at all but the result of too much rum and too many financial problems.

One of the witnesses said it had been a typical New Year's Eve.

"We did our annual dance on the bar," she said.

You were feeling no pain? asked Hoag.

"Nobody fell off," she said.

That's for the jury to decide, I thought.

TRIAL IS REMINDER: SOMETIMES, NICE PEOPLE DO STUPID THINGS

5.20.2007

Perhaps because so many of us are doomed to lose it, men don't care enough about their hair to become close to the people who cut it, but women are almost always friends with their stylists. Certainly, Debbie Masten was close to the two women who owned the beauty salon she patronized.

Both were at the 2004 New Year's Eve party at Masten's bar in Kirksville, Too Tall Two Eatery & Spirits. Not long after the party ended, a passer-by noticed flames and called 911. Investigators traced the source of the fire to a bag of papers and declared that the fire had been intentionally set. Masten was charged with arson. Because the business involved interstate commerce, federal authorities took jurisdiction.

At the time of the fire, Masten was the mayor of Kirksville. She owned a popular saloon. She had a nice circle of friends. Why would she set her saloon on fire?

The feds quickly learned that the saloon was not doing well. In fact, it was a financial disaster. In its last three years, it had lost about $238,000. Masten had not been paying taxes, and the IRS was after her. Checks to suppliers were bouncing. So yes, there was a motive for arson, but even a good motive didn't answer the next question: Why would an intelligent woman set fire to her saloon in the early morning hours of Jan. 1?

If a person's intent is to burn a building, why not start the fire in the early morning hours of a Wednesday in mid-January? The streets would be deserted. The fire would have a chance to get going. Evidence like a bag of papers would be destroyed. But New Year's Eve? The night of the year that almost everybody stays up late? That would be the worst possible night.

That seemed to be the best argument for the defense. An intelligent woman would not have picked this time to do something like this. And Masten is intelligent. No question about that.

She was on the witness stand Wednesday, and she did very well when she was questioned by her attorney, Douglas Forsyth. Yes, there had been some financial problems, but things were getting better. And if she wanted to get rid of the bar, she could have sold it. In fact, she was thinking of doing just that at the time of the fire.

She did not do so well under cross-examination by Assistant U.S. Attorney Dean Hoag. He reminded me of a boxer. He'd home in on one topic – jab, jab, jab – and then switch to another – jab, jab, jab – and then go back to the first. He kept Masten off-balance. She survived, but a prosecutor doesn't need a knock-out. A unanimous decision is enough.

The facts of the case were on the side of the government. The financial problems were clear. Except for one expert hired by the defense, everybody agreed that the fire had been set. Masten was the last person to leave the bar. Only minutes after she left the bar, a passer-by noticed the fire.

But why do this on New Year's Eve? In what was more of a statement than a question, Hoag concluded his cross-examination: It wasn't that the buyer backed out, you were up to your neck in debt and you had too much to drink so you set your bar on fire, was it? No, said Masten.

Earlier, though, her friends, the stylists, had testified about a fun and hard-drinking night that had concluded with a dance on the bar. I wrote about that and got an e-mail from a young man who wrote that he'd been at Too Tall that night. "By the time we arrived, Debbie was already inebriated and dancing around like a crazy person. I remember her grabbing me by my tie and dancing with me. She proceeded to slap me on the rear, to which I remember thinking (and saying), 'I can't believe this person is the mayor.' What a night!"

What a night, indeed. I liked Masten and her friends, not only the stylists, but also the other folks who came to the trial to support her. But I figured Hoag had it right in his last question. It was heartbreaking to imagine Masten, unable to think clearly and reflect upon what she was doing, making a spur-of-the-moment decision, dousing some paper with 151 rum, setting it afire and then walking out into the cold night. So foolish, so out of character.

She now faces a minimum of five years in prison.

I remember talking to a defense lawyer some years ago. His client had done something incredibly stupid, and I mentioned that fact to the lawyer.

"That's true of all my clients," he said. "If people weren't capable of doing stupid things, I wouldn't have any clients."

WITH MEDIUM MAC, SUSPEND DISBELIEF

1.13.2010

Five years ago next month, the newspaper received the following statement from Big Mac: "Once and for all, I did not use steroids or any other illegal substance."

Now we have a newer version of truth from the smaller Medium Mac. He did use steroids, but only for his health, never to enhance his performance. For that matter, the steroids did not help him hit all those home runs. That ability was a gift from God. Nevertheless, Medium Mac is sorry about taking steroids.

Why would you be sorry you did something for your health? That's like apologizing for eating vegetables.

Also, we have learned that Tony La Russa, the smartest man in baseball and Mark McGwire's staunchest defender, learned only this week that his longtime friend was a steroid user. "Mark and I never confronted it," he told ESPN.

Not even after Jose Canseco's book about rampant steroid use among La Russa's Oakland players, a book in which Canseco specifically mentioned McGwire? Not even after Big Mac went to Congress and refused to talk about the past?

At a time when everybody in baseball was talking about McGwire and steroids, and La Russa was front and center denying all such allegations, it never came up?

What are we to make of all this?

I think of that famous sportswriter, Samuel Taylor Coleridge. Back in 1817, he wrote that being a baseball fan in the steroid era requires a "willing suspension of disbelief." Actually, Coleridge was writing about a reader's responsibility to accept supernatural elements – witches and such – as part of what he called poetic faith.

But he could have been talking about baseball in the steroid era.

A home run record that had been almost sacred and unapproachable was suddenly demolished. And not just by Big Mac. Sammy Sosa hit 66 home runs the same year.

In hindsight, it's easy to say we should have known. And maybe we did. Remember the reporter finding the Andro in Big Mac's locker? That's called a clue.

Most people ignored it. In fact, the villain in that story was the snoopy reporter.

So we're good at this suspension of disbelief thing.

That's good news for Medium Mac. He's got a tough story to sell now. He sees himself as a victim. He said he's sorry he played in the steroid era. He said he wishes there had been drug testing when he started playing.

It's as if Bernie Madoff were lamenting the lack of regulation that allowed him to swindle investors.

Actually, Big Mac's home runs and Madoff's fantastic returns have a common theme. If something seems too good to be true, it probably is. But just as it must have been fun if you were on the top of the Ponzi scheme to get those outsized returns, it was fun to watch the super-sized Big Mac swat those long, long flies.

Medium Mac says he's happy he now has the opportunity to talk about the past. Exactly why he didn't feel he had the same opportunity last year or the year before is something I don't understand. What we do know is that Medium Mac owes this particular opportunity to La Russa, who named him hitting coach.

La Russa deserves some credit for that. He might be the most uncurious man in baseball, but for a man whose legacy is tied to steroids – his Oakland clubhouse seems to have been ground zero – he has never run from the subject. Just the opposite. When Barry Bonds was radioactive to everybody else, La Russa talked about bringing him to St. Louis. Most recently, he has talked about another tainted player, Miguel Tejada.

That sits well with the parishioners of the Church of the Second Chance. We like to say we're all liars and cheaters and scoundrels to one degree or another. As far as Medium Mac is concerned, we normally prefer an apology to contain an admission of error, but we're not sticklers about that. We're always ready to forgive.

The baseball fans of St. Louis will be even more enthusiastic. Medium Mac might make an appearance this weekend at the Cardinals' annual Winter Warm-Up. If he does, the fans will pour love all over him. It won't matter that his accomplishments here were essentially fraudulent or that his long home runs were chemically induced. It won't matter that he used to catch the first flight out of town at season's end.

No, it's the middle of winter. The thought of baseball is intoxicating. Green grass, the crack of a bat striking a ball. The fans are ready to willingly suspend disbelief. Big Mac was a favorite. We'll like Medium Mac even more.

A FAMILY'S TITANIC MIRACLE LIVES ON

4.12.2009

Eugene Daly was born in 1883 in the town of Athlone in central Ireland. His father was a policeman, who was sent north to Belfast in the summer of 1895 to help keep the peace during the Protestant marches that marked the anniversary of the Battle of the Boyne.

As often happened, a riot broke out during a march. Bricks were thrown. One struck Officer Daly in the head. He died. So Eugene became the head of the family at age 12. He went to work in the woolen mills that lined the banks of the River Shannon that cut through the town of Athlone.

Seventeen years later, with his younger siblings grown, Daly decided to immigrate to America. On April 11, 1912, he boarded the RMS Titanic in Queenstown in County Cork. He had a third-class ticket.

In the book, "The Irish Aboard the Titanic," author Senan Molony wrote that Daly was a musician who played the bagpipes as the immigrants waited to board. These Irish immigrants were a lively bunch, and Daly knew the jigs and reels to which they danced. Did he play at the parties below the decks? Almost certainly.

On the night of the 14th, he was jolted awake in his cramped quarters in steerage. He grabbed his heavy black coat and headed out to see what was going on. "Go back to bed," said a passing steward, but Daly ignored him. A cousin and one of her friends, both from Athlone, also were traveling third-class, and Daly had promised their folks he'd look out for them. So he woke them, and led them up the stairs.

By the time they reached the upper deck, it was clear that things weren't all right. They had to fight their way to the lifeboats. Eugene got his cousin and her friend in one of the boats and then tried to get in himself. He was pulled back. "Women and children only," somebody shouted.

Eugene saw a ship's officer shoot two men. Across the deck, a canvas craft was stuck under a wire stay which ran up to the mast. Men were trying to free the craft. Eugene joined them. Then the ship lurched hard and the water washed Eugene off the deck. The same surge of water freed the canvas boat. Eugene grabbed on to it. All around people were screaming. He hung on.

The screaming stopped. Eugene hung on. Eventually, a lifeboat came back looking for survivors. Eugene was dragged aboard. Much later, the Carpathia arrived on the scene.

After a series of jobs in New York, Eugene got a job as a mechanic with the Otis Elevator Company in New Jersey. One of his friends at Otis had a sister, Lil. She worked as a personal companion for a rich woman. So Lil was relatively well-to-do, and traveled to Ireland almost every year to visit her parents. In the spring of 1915, Lil bought a ticket to Ireland, but when her wealthy benefactor had a change in plans, Liz had to cancel her booking. Thus, she was not on the Lusitania when it sailed in early May.

Eugene enlisted in the Army for World War I, and proposed to Lil. "Sure the poor devil was going off to war and I thought I'd never see him again so I accepted his proposal," she said later. Eugene never left the states. Lil quit her job, and the couple settled in a cold-water flat in Brooklyn.

In 1921, they got news that Eugene's mother was gravely ill. They went to Ireland to see her. The trip over was very difficult for Eugene. To Lil's chagrin, he swore never to set foot on a ship again. They settled in Galway. Eugene got a job in a woolen mill.

In 1925, they had a daughter, Mary. At night when she was cold, her father would take a heavy old coat and put it over her. It was the coat he had worn on the Titanic. It had a greenish tinge, and she used to wonder if the color came from the sea.

Mary fell in love with a young man, Michael Joyce. He was a wonderful singer. They were married in 1946, and in 1952, they moved to this country. Michael hoped to be the next great Irish tenor.

But that didn't work out – rock and roll was the next big thing – and Michael got a job in a warehouse. He and Mary reared 10 children in the Bronx. In 1961, Lil died, and Eugene agreed to return to America to live with Mary and her family. He took an airplane across the Atlantic.

He was something of an oddity in the Bronx. Armed only with his cane, he would casually saunter across the busiest of streets. When an impatient motorist would honk, he'd rap on the hood of the car with his cane. "What's your hurry? When God made time, he made plenty of it."

He died of natural causes in 1965.

In 1989, Mary and Michael moved to Union, about 50 miles southwest of St.

Louis. One of their sons, Michael, is a police officer in Union.

The elder Michael died in 1991, and Mary lives alone, just down the street from her son. She has no relics from the Titanic – she doesn't know what happened to her father's coat – and there are no signs that she is the child of a survivor of the great disaster. But she has 32 grandchildren and 10 great-grandchildren, and she believes that each one of them is something of a miracle. "God watched over my father on that long ago night," she told me.

CHILD PORNOGRAPHY CASES: MEASURING THE TIME FOR THE CRIME

11.9.2008

On the morning of Halloween, Mark Shklar came into federal court in an orange jumpsuit, dressed as a prisoner. At least, it seemed like a costume.

He was, at least officially, still a member in good standing of the Missouri Bar Association. The middle rows in the courtroom were filled with his supporters, including his ex-wife and his 21-year-old son. Both spoke movingly on his behalf. So did a couple of attorneys. This is a good and decent man, they said. Then Shklar spoke. He said he was lucky to have family and friends like these. Then the judge sentenced him to 41 months in prison for possession of child pornography.

Carrie Costantin, the assistant U.S. attorney who handled the case, was almost wistful when I spoke with her later.

"The supporters are almost never there when these guys plead guilty," she said. "That's when we go into what they're really pleading guilty to. Instead, they show up for sentencing. It's like we're talking past each other."

Things were more graphic on the day in October when Shklar pleaded guilty. Costantin made it clear that Shklar had not inadvertently downloaded child pornography. He had sought it out on his computer. He had downloaded 24 such videos. The six mentioned in the indictment involved images of preteens.

Still, even on that day, Shklar did not seem like a monster. We spoke in the hallway outside of the courtroom. He was dressed casually. He carried a little plastic bag with his medications. He was ready to go to jail, where he would await official sentencing.

I had met Shklar some time earlier. He had been busted, but not yet indicted. He told me he was 58 and divorced. He didn't date. In the privacy of his apartment, he watched pornography. Eventually, he found child pornography. He mainly watched the adult stuff, but sometimes he searched out the forbidden images of children. He got everything through a file sharing service, so he rationalized that because he wasn't paying for it, he wasn't really supporting the industry.

One day there was a banging at his door. Armed men wearing helmets and visors pushed their way in. Shklar at first thought it was a mistake. He figured they must be looking for drugs. When they told him they were there to look for child pornography on his computer, he realized that the world as he had known it was about to change.

But he had not expected that he would automatically go to prison. Nor had he imagined that the feds could use the fact that he obtained the child pornography through a file sharing system as an enhancement at sentencing. File sharing translates into distribution.

He hired defense attorney Joel Schwartz. "This is the kind of case I hate," Schwartz said. "There is really nothing I can do for him."

Schwartz did as well as could be expected. Had the feds pushed the enhancement with the file sharing system, Shklar could have gotten 96 months.

After meeting Shklar, I started paying attention to these cases. I was surprised to learn that people generally get more time for possession of child pornography than they do for molesting a child. Costantin, who used to work as a county prosecutor, explained that to me. When a person is charged with molesting a child, the defense knows that the parents of the child generally do not want to subject the child to the trauma of testifying, so the defense has an advantage during plea negotiations. In child pornography cases, the defense does not want the jury to see the images or the videos, so the advantage goes to the government.

Perhaps the oddest sentencing I saw was in August when 77-year-old Roderick McArthur received a sentence of 151 months for possession of child pornography. He hobbled into the courtroom hunched over a walker. He was with his wife and daughter. He was given the severe sentence because of his record. In 1986, he had pleaded guilty to child sodomy after inappropriately touching a child. He was given probation. He came to the attention of authorities again in 2006 when a mall security guard spotted him in his car inappropriately touching himself. He was arrested for public indecency. He had a lewd drawing of a child in his wallet. Shortly thereafter, police searched his computer and found the forbidden images. Before his sentencing, McArthur told me he watched a lot of pornography, but no child pornography. He said he didn't know how those images got on his computer.

I am no expert on the "normal" sexual drive of a 77-year-old, but McArthur struck me as abnormal. But should his abnormality result in a life sentence in prison?

Of course, McArthur was the exception. Many of the defendants were closer to Shklar. He had no record. In fact, he had the opposite of a record. He seemed to be respected by everybody.

I talked to a police officer who investigates these things, and he emphasized the fact that these are not victimless crimes. These are real kids, he said. Imagine that this is happening on a stage in an illicit theater, he said, and the people who watch this stuff are all in the audience.

That puts it in a different light, I suppose, but a lot of these fellows wouldn't seek out the theater. They only watch because they can do it in the supposed privacy of their homes. The computer makes it easy.

In fact, as the marshals led Shklar out of the courtroom, I thought of "2001: A Space Odyssey." The computer, Hal, took over the spacecraft. I wish I had asked Shklar if he had ever seen that movie.

UNINSURED WOMAN GOT TOP CARE, THEN GOT ARRESTED

9.17.2006

Tichelle Whaley is a certified nursing assistant. She works in retirement homes, caring for the elderly and the disabled. It is not always pleasant work and sometimes difficult. It does not pay a lot.

In February 2004, she was in the midst of some difficult times. She had two young children. Her husband was in prison. She had quit one job in January – that job did not offer health insurance – and had started a new job. She would eventually get health insurance with the new job, but it had not yet kicked in. And she was feeling sick. She tried to work through it, but she kept feeling worse and worse.

One of her sisters was also working as a nursing assistant. She had health insurance. When Tichelle started having severe abdominal pains one day, she used her sister's identification and went to DePaul Hospital.

"I'm not a hospital person," she told me Friday. "I'm not sickly. I really figured I'd just go to the emergency room and be in and out."

Instead, she was diagnosed with severe acute necrotizing pancreatitis, a condition caused by previous bouts of gallstones. At any rate, she was very ill. She was admitted to the hospital and she remained there for almost a month as doctors fought to stabilize her.

She was, of course, being treated under her sister's insurance. That was wrong and Tichelle knew it, but once you get on this roller coaster, how do you get off? Besides, she was 26, she had two small children and she was afraid she might die. At the time, legal problems seemed the least of her worries.

She was released from the hospital in mid-March, but two days later was admitted to Christian Hospital Northeast, again under the name of her sister. She was transferred to Barnes-Jewish Hospital. She underwent surgery. She was put into a medically induced coma. "I went to sleep and the next thing I knew, it was three and a half weeks later, and I had tubes everywhere," she said. She spent days on a ventilator. She had a life-threatening staph infection, which led to pneumonia. She received numerous transfusions.

In other words, she received top-of-the-line care at a world-class hospital. All told, she spent 47 days at Barnes, much of it in critical condition and much of it in an intensive care unit. Thanks to all of this care, she survived.

It was, needless to say, very expensive care, and when the insurance company called the nursing home where Tichelle's sister worked to verify certain things and learned that Tichelle's sister had not been in the hospital, the deception quickly unraveled. Tichelle's sister lost her job, and Tichelle was arrested. She was charged with fraud. The official charge was felony misuse of a Social Security account number.

The federal criminal justice system relies heavily on sentencing guidelines. The severity of the crime and the defendant's criminal history are the salient points. On criminal history, Tichelle was fine. She had none. But the size of the fraud was against her. The medical bills totaled more than $400,000. Sort of, anyway. It is an oddity of our health care system that the medical bills and the cost to the insurance company are two different things. Insurance companies pay a good deal less than 100 cents on the dollar. In this instance, the insurance company would have paid only about half the official bill.

The bottom line is Tichelle owed about $259,000.

She pleaded guilty last month and came to court Friday for sentencing. Her husband and their youngest child came, too. All were dressed as if going to church. Tichelle's husband had been released from prison during her stay at Barnes.

The guidelines called for a sentence of 18 to 24 months. Federal public defender Tom Flynn had filed a motion requesting a downward departure from the guidelines, and he argued on behalf of that motion Friday morning. He said circumstances had caused the fraud. She acted out of desperation, Flynn said. Assistant U.S. Attorney Tom Albus told the judge that the government had no objection to a downward departure from the guidelines. Flynn pointed out that his client had returned to work and he argued that incarceration would serve no purpose. Albus added that the government considered the chance of recidivism in this case to be very low.

U.S. District Court Judge Rodney Sipple listened to the two lawyers and nodded. He said he didn't see the need for incarceration. He then sentenced Tichelle to five years probation and ordered her to pay $259,000 in restitution. She is supposed to pay $100 a month.

I spoke with her after court. She said the damage to her pancreas has caused diabetes, but otherwise her health is good. She said she would like to go back to school and learn to be a respiratory therapist, but she is not sure if that is possible with a felony on her record. She was on Medicaid after her hospitalization and arrest, but as soon as she recovered, she went back to work and she is again working as a nursing assistant. She makes too much to be eligible for Medicaid, and while her new job offers health insurance, enrollment is closed until November. She said she inquired about private health insurance, but her health history and her diabetes make the costs prohibitive.

For the moment, then, she is again without health insurance.

FREE COFFEE, FREE NEWS, BUT THESE POLICIES COST US

2.2.2009

During the week I make my own coffee, but on the weekends, I walk to the neighborhood coffee shop and order a couple of lattes to go. The shop has "coffee club" cards. Eleven punches and the next one is free. On Saturday, I ordered my two lattes to go, paid for them, and then handed the young barista – a new kid, I hadn't seen him before – my coffee club card. He punched it once and handed it back.

"I bought two lattes," I said.

"Yessir, but it says right on the card, 'One punch per visit.'"

"You mean I get the same credit whether I buy one latte or twelve of them? That makes no sense," I said.

"It's the policy," he said.

Actually, I am well aware of that. In fact, I have something of a reputation for making a fuss about the policy. On occasion, I have even ranted about it. "What are you? A mindless drone? Forget about the damned policy and do what you know is right!"

There are a couple of baristas who automatically punch my card twice. Maybe they figure life is hard enough without me making a scene. Or maybe they have a heightened sense of right and wrong. Who cares? I give them my card. Punch. Punch.

"You're a Jedi warrior," I say. "Down with the Empire. Power to the people."

"Whatever you say, Miles."

That's what I'm known as at the coffee shop. Kind of a long story, but to be short about it, whenever I go some place for a takeout order, I use the name Miles. Sometimes when my order is ready, the person will holler, "Miles! To go!" At

which point I holler back, "Before I sleep!"

I live for those moments.

That is an affliction I have. I am a completely normal person who likes to appear odd. I see this affliction at universities, most often in English departments. People who are perfectly normal go out of their way to appear abnormal. Sometimes they wear patches on their elbows. Sometimes the men wear ponytails. It's as if there is something wrong with being normal.

It used to be easier to appear odd. For instance, I talk to myself. Sometimes loudly. It used to bother my children. "Dad, have you ever noticed that when you go for your walks, people sometimes cross the street when they see you coming? Especially if you're yelling and waving your arms."

Those were the good old days. Now it's common to see a person talking to himself. But not really. If you look closely, you'll see that the person has a device in his ear. He's on the phone.

For some reason, this bugs me. The other day, I was on an elevator in a downtown building and some man was just jabbering away. "This is probably some latte-sipping liberal who made a big deal about Bush and Cheney wanting to eavesdrop on Americans," I thought to myself. "Like privacy is a big deal to this person." Suddenly, he looked over at me and did a double take. He recognized me. "Excuse me," he said to his unseen co-conspirator. And then to me, "Hey, aren't you Miles from the coffee shop?"

Truth is, I'm proud to be recognized as Miles from the coffee shop. Yes, I sometimes make a scene, but I'm doing those young baristas a favor. You don't want to be the kind of person who follows "the policy." I've had it with those kind of people. When I went in to the Revenue Office to get license plates for my car, the clerk said, "I need a copy of your application for the title." I said, "I can do better than that. I brought the actual title." She said, "I need the application for the title." I said, "Why do I have to prove I applied for the title when I have the title?" She said, "It's the policy."

I am not going to argue about the economics of the coffee shop's policy. Buy eleven, get one free. To make it economically viable, you charge an eleventh more per drink. Basically, what you're trying to do with this policy is generate goodwill among your steadiest customers. The last thing you want to do is alienate one. When I buy two lattes and get credit for one, I'm alienated.

Admittedly, this newspaper does not give away every twelfth newspaper. Wait a minute. We give the whole thing away. You can read it for nothing on the Internet.

It's not just us, of course. The other day I was talking with Wendy Wiese, a colleague from Channel 9's "Donnybrook." She said something about AmerenUE, and I said, "That's interesting. Where did you learn that?" She said, "The Business Journal." I said, "You subscribe?" She said, "No, I read it online." "When did you read it?" I asked. She said, "Wednesday."

I do subscribe to the Business Journal. I get my copy in the mail on Friday. So I am paying to read on Friday what Wendy read for free on Wednesday.

I get complaints from people all the time. Last week I got a letter from Mary H. "I'm just so sick and tired of reading, 'To find out more, log on to STLtoday.com.' I don't want to! That's why I'm reading this, you morons!"

Also last week, I was at the courthouse, and a friend stopped me. "I don't know why I still subscribe," he said. "I get the feeling you guys are putting more and more resources into the Internet and paying less and less attention to the people who actually buy the paper. Why should somebody who doesn't pay get more than somebody who pays?"

I sighed. "It's the policy," I said.

He shook his head. I turned and walked out of the courthouse. I was talking to myself as I walked, of course, but nobody seemed to think it was odd.

LEAD IN SOIL: HAZARD OR SUSTENANCE?

1.18.2009

A soil technician from the Doe Run Company visited Bearl and Grace Carrow at their home on Young Street in Bonne Terre, Mo., this past week.

He was there to get some papers signed because the company is required by the Environmental Protection Agency to "obtain all necessary access agreements to conduct residential yard sampling and, if specific criteria are met, residential soil removals in specific areas of St. Francois County."

In other words, the federal government has told Doe Run that the company is supposed to check the soil for lead, and if the concentration of lead is high enough, the company is supposed to remove that soil.

The soil around the Carrow home has already been tested, and the EPA has determined that the concentration of lead is high enough that the soil to a depth of 12 inches should be removed. Twelve inches of new soil will be brought in. Grass will be planted.

You might think the Carrows would be happy. The government is looking after them. Instead, the Carrows are somewhere between bemused and agitated.

"Actually, they're resigned," said Betty Hoffee, one of their daughters.

The Carrows celebrated their 72nd wedding anniversary in December. They met in first grade in a little school in French Village, which was hardly even a village back in those days before World War I. Bearl came from a farm family. Grace was born in St. Louis and spent the first four years of her life in the city. Her dad hauled coal in the winter and ice in the summer. Then his health went bad and the family moved to the country. He did odd jobs.

Shortly after Grace finished first grade, her family moved from French Village to the much larger Bonne Terre. Some years later, when she was 23, her sister's boyfriend introduced her to Bearl. Technically, he reintroduced her to Bearl, but the truth is, Grace did not remember Bearl from first grade.

Two years later, they were married.

Bearl became a miner for the St. Joseph Lead Company, the predecessor to Doe Run. He worked long hours underground. One of his specialities was called "cutting drift." He worked on a trapeze, suspended about 30 feet above the mine floor. He would dig into the wall of the mine with a drill, and then he'd put dynamite into the hole he'd just dug. The resultant explosions could be heard above ground. In fact, the whole town would shake a little bit, almost as if it were experiencing an earthquake.

It was dangerous work. "I had some close escapes," Bearl told me. He worked in the mines for 32 years. He retired in 1972, when the lead mines in St. Francois County closed.

Grace and Bearl had four children – Lois, Kathy, Betty and Don. They were raised in the house on Young Street where the Carrows have lived since 1942. As children, they played on the "chat" hill across the street. Chat is a term for the waste from the mine.

The children now range in age from 61 to 71.

"We used to play with the core samples from the mine," said Don, the youngest of the children. He now lives across the street from his parents.

The family had a large garden in the backyard. They raised corn, potatoes, tomatoes, onions, green beans, lettuce and beets. In addition to helping feed the family, it was a labor of love for Bearl. The family says he was always out there digging in the dirt. Grace would can the vegetables so they could be served all winter.

So you can imagine how the family felt about what they considered the "good earth" of Bonne Terre. It sustained them. And how could they be afraid of the lead? It provided their father's livelihood.

Still, the EPA was concerned about the concentration of lead in the soil. In 1997, Doe Run entered into an agreement with the EPA to check the soil. Sometime later – the Carrows think it was 2001 – people came around to test their soil.

The Carrows were not surprised that it passed.

In 2007, the Carrows were informed that the lead levels in their yard were high enough to qualify for removal. The family was uncertain what to do. Bearl and Grace were in their 90s. Having their entire yard dug up seemed like an ordeal. On the other hand, the house and property would be forever unmarketable if they did nothing after the government had declared the lead levels dangerously high. The people at Doe Run were reasonable. The removal could be delayed if the forms weren't returned promptly, but eventually the family would have to decide yes or no.

I visited the Carrows last week shortly before they signed the papers. In addition to Bearl and Grace, both of whom will be 97 in May (Bearl is two days older than Grace), Kathy, Betty and Don were at the house. Everybody looked good. Any health problems? No, they said. If this is what lead does to you, I thought, maybe we ought to put some in the water.

Later, I called John Carter. He is the project manager for Doe Run on the St. Francois County lead project. I told him the Carrows had a garden. How can that soil be dangerous?

"I've heard these questions before," he said. He explained that it's all a matter of numbers. The EPA has set standards for how much lead can be in residential yard soil, and those standards are geared for children from 6 months to 6 years.

The Carrow kids, two of whom are in their 70s, were raised on that soil, I said. "Some children are more sensitive than others," he said.

He also explained the changing standards. The first agreement that Doe Run signed called for the removal of soil that had a certain level of lead. After that soil had been removed, the company negotiated another agreement to remove soil with a lesser concentration, soil that was still considered potentially dangerous.

The Carrows' soil will be removed sometime this spring. It will not affect the garden. Bearl quit gardening in 2007, after suffering a stroke.

HOW CLOSE A SHAMEFUL MEMORY WAS TO A TRAGEDY

3.14.2008

Three young men decided to go to New Orleans and look for work. I say "young men" with some reluctance. Is an 18-year-old really a man? "Old enough to go to war but not old enough to drink." In this instance, that old saying was beside the point. All three of these young men drank. Much of the time they drank more than they should, which is the way of it for most 18-year-olds who drink.

The night before they left, they went to a party. They were drinking. They did not know many of the people at the party. The girls at the party had left their coats and purses in a bedroom. One of the three young men, all of whom came from stable, middle-class families, decided it would be cool to go through the purses and see if there was any money. He recruited one of the others to help. The third, not quite gutsy enough to do the stealing himself, agreed to be the lookout. That was me.

But I was a poor lookout, and one of the girls noticed my friends going through the purses. She let out a scream. My friends and I rushed out of the house, jumped into our car and raced away. The guy who was driving (not me) didn't hit anybody on the way out, and so that was that. We continued on to New Orleans.

That is one of the seediest things I've ever done, but certainly not the most stupid. I shudder when I think about the stupid things I've done. I take limited solace in the fact that I am not alone. If it weren't for luck, few males would reach the age of 25.

Eventually, though, we do reach 25 and then 30, and for the most part, our really stupid days are behind us. In fact, we put them out of our minds. I had not even thought about the long ago party and the purses until good Samaritan Roger Kreutz was killed when he tried to intervene in the theft of a tip jar at a coffee shop in Crestwood.

"Would you have done that?" a friend asked, and I answered, "I might have," and although my friend was asking if I would have done what Kreutz did, I was actually answering that I could have been on both sides. I could have been the 19-year-old stealing the tip jar. A lookout, anyway. On the other hand, the older me could have been the adult refusing to just stand there and let it happen.

I'm not trying to engender sympathy for the 19-year-old, Aaron Poisson. With luck, he would have gotten away and his road trip and his life would have continued. The theft of a tip jar would become a fuzzy and shameful memory. But luck deserted him, and he'll have to pay the consequences. The system owes that to his victim.

I said that when we reach 30, we generally manage to forget the stupid things we once did. That's not quite true. We think of them again, albeit in a general way, when our kids get to be teenagers. We look at our children, especially our sons, and we think, "Don't make the same mistakes I did."

But life changes little, if at all. Young men continue to do foolish things. Drinking is right there at the top of the list. Teens drink and drink irresponsibly. Maybe if we were as sophisticated as the Europeans and let kids drink wine with dinner, they would learn to drink responsibly. Who knows? As it is now, we hold our breath and hope for luck.

Or sometimes we yell. That is what Larry Doss did. By all accounts, his 18-year-old son Casey drinks like most 18-year-olds do, which is recklessly. He was drunk when he came home at 4 a.m. on Feb. 24. His father yelled at him, blocked the door to his bedroom. Ostensibly, the father was angry about the muffler on his son's car, but most parents can imagine that the muffler was not the real source of concern.

Post-Dispatch reporter Joel Currier talked to Shirley Doss, the wife and mother, and documented what happened next. The father and son struggled, fell down the stairs, and the fight continued in the living room. Shirley called the police. They took Casey away. Shirley and Larry were going to get their son out of jail in the morning. But Larry lost consciousness after he went to bed. He was taking a blood thinner to prevent clotting of the arteries, and the blows to his head apparently caused hemorrhaging around his brain. He died. His son, who reportedly remembers little about the event, has been charged with involuntary manslaughter.

What should the criminal justice system do in this case? I suspect the victim would be the strongest voice for mercy.

Bill McClellan • Gently Down the Stream

PASSPORT SHOP THRIVES OUT OF STEP

2.17.2010

I am a regular customer at the passport photo shop just west of Big Bend on Clayton Road. That means I visit every 10 years and spend a few bucks to get photos for a new passport.

Dan Hoadley, the proprietor of the shop, also repairs clocks. How often do people need that service? Probably less often than they need new passport photos.

Although I understand little about economics, I wonder about the business model.

The other day, I stopped by the Mobil gas station that sits in the middle of Clayton Road just west of Big Bend. The franchise has belonged to the Steinrauf family since 1974. Although the station has always looked busy to me, the family is losing the franchise next month.

I heard that news and I thought about the Parkmoor restaurant that used to sit at the northeast corner of the intersection. It was a landmark from 1930 to 1999. Now it's just a memory, and its old site is part of a Walgreens parking lot.

Somehow, the passport photo shop survives. A large sign overhangs the sidewalk. "Passport," it says, although, of course, you can't actually get a passport there. For that, you have to go to the post office. By the way, the post office does passport photos. For that matter, so does Walgreens.

I stopped by Monday to visit Hoadley. It was a little after noon. He had had two customers that morning. They did not need standard passport photos but photos for United Kingdom driver licenses. The specifications for those are a little different.

Hoadley explained that he gets a lot of business like that. For instance, foreign nationals who need passport photos often require something a little different. Who would know the precise size required for a Moroccan passport? Or who would know which countries don't accept a photo in which the person is smiling?

Hoadley knows these things. That word has gotten around. Nobody keeps statistics, but Hoadley figures he gets most of the foreign business in the St. Louis area.

He got started in the photography business in his hometown of French Lick, Ind. That is basketball player Larry Bird's hometown, too, and Hoadley went to high school with Bird. But while Bird went off to play college basketball, Hoadley stayed in French Lick working at a hotel that offered complimentary photographs for its guests. Hoadley was the photographer.

Later, he did standard portrait photos and wedding photos, but shortly after he moved here to work as a portrait photographer, he went into business for himself. That was in 1981. He specialized in passport photos.

In those days, he used Polaroid film. He charged $6.99. In the next 20 years, he had raised his price to $9.99. But then came digital photography, and all of the aforementioned competition. He is back to charging $6.99. That is a dollar less than Walgreens charges, and less than half what the post office charges.

Furthermore, he told me his photos are higher quality. "I still have the lighting I needed for Polaroid. I don't need that kind of lighting for digital, but it makes for better photos."

Of course, there are people who don't care about quality. If they're strictly into convenience, they might go to the closest place. If they're strictly into price, they might take their own photos.

Hoadley is there for people who are old-fashioned enough to care.

You could say something similar about clocks. We've become a throwaway society. Not many people care enough about a clock to get it repaired.

Hoadley does, of course. He has always collected old clocks, and if you collect them, you better learn how to repair them. So that became part of the business. It is, in a sense, a business from another time.

"People who have wind-up clocks have already stepped back from this age," Hoadley said. "We're helping people get back something that they've lost."

On the day I visited, Gary Stevenson, a retired schoolteacher, was in the shop working on an ancient phonograph. "There is a certain beauty in mechanical music," said Stevenson.

He and Hoadley are old friends. They share similar tastes in music. They both have antique grind organs. In fact, if you went to the Barkus Parade in Soulard last week, you might have seen Hoadley marching with his grind organ and his dog, Storm. This was their 13th consecutive appearance at the parade. Hoadley, who is single, worries about Storm. She is 14, and her health is failing.

While I was there, it turned 1 o'clock, and clocks began to chime. Time passes, but for some people the old ways remain.

"It's a tough business world," said Hoadley, "but somebody with stamina can still thrive."

Bill McClellan • Gently Down the Stream

YOU CAN HAVE INSURANCE AND STILL END UP $90,000 IN DEBT

5.13.2007

Two bill collectors called Gary Heller on Monday. "That is the first time anything like that ever happened to me," he said. He sounded almost dumbfounded.

Heller is not accustomed to owing anybody anything. He has solid, small-town values. He spent the first eight years of his life in the Illinois town of Red Bud. Then his parents moved down the road to Sparta, and there he has stayed ever since. He is now 54 years old.

He met the love of his life at Sparta High School. He and Teri went out for the first time on Halloween night of 1969. They went to the town parade, and that was that. They were a couple. They graduated from high school. They got married. They started a family. Eventually, they had three children. Gary had a series of jobs as a mechanic before finally getting a job at Spartan Printing Inc. The printing plant was the largest employer in Randolph County. The pay was decent, and the benefits were excellent.

Teri worked a series of jobs, too. She was a waitress. She sold Mary Kay products. She worked in a grocery store. Then the Hellers bought the roller skating rink in town, and Teri ran that.

In 1996, Spartan Printing shut down.

In a sense, Heller was a little part of a big story. Factories and plants were shutting down all over America. Blue-collar workers were feeling the effects of globalization.

Heller went back into the Great Hustle. He did home repair work. He got a water delivery route. Eventually, he became the authorized retailer for a satellite television company.

None of these new jobs provided health insurance.

Fortunately, the three kids were grown. The youngest was 21 when Spartan Printing shut its doors. Still, health insurance for just Gary and Teri was not cheap. Actually, it wasn't so bad in 1996. His first policy on the open market had been from Country Insurance. Then Country sold its health insurance policies to Blue Cross and Blue Shield. Heller was pleased. But by 2006, his premiums had risen to more than $600 a month.

Once again, Heller was a little part of a big story. Health insurance was becoming too expensive for many working people.

Heller began looking for a cheaper policy. He found a company called Assurant Health.

A salesman came and talked to him. Heller could get a policy for himself and Teri for a total cost of $293 a month. That was less than half of what he was paying.

The rate was guaranteed for the first year. There was a $2 million lifetime benefit for each covered person, a calendar-year maximum of $250,000 per covered person, an annual prescription drug maximum of $250,000 per covered person and an outpatient calendar year maximum of $5,000 per covered person. There was an annual individual deductible of $2,500, and additional non-network deductibles. The coverage included one air or ground ambulance service to the nearest hospital per year with a maximum limited to $1,000.

To an unsophisticated consumer, it seemed pretty reasonable. Heller switched policies in February 2006. He received a letter from Assurant Health in March. "Thank you for choosing us for your health insurance needs. You have selected one of the finest health care plans in the industry."

A couple of months later, Teri felt a pain in her side. Then she had a lump in her neck, and then a lump in her chest. In June, she had a CAT scan. She had cancer. She had another CAT scan, a biopsy, a PET scan and an MRI.

All of this, of course, was done on an outpatient basis. Remember the outpatient calendar year maximum of $5,000? Within a matter of days, she was over her limit.

The good news is that no care was denied to her. The bad news is she understood that the insurance company was not covering her care. Even as her health deteriorated, she worried that she was pushing her husband toward bankruptcy.

Heller complained to the Illinois Division of Insurance, but his complaint was denied. Assurant had not violated the terms of its policy.

Teri died three months ago. Heller still owes almost $90,000.

I called Assurant Health. Peter Duckler from HLB Communications called me back. Assurant Health will not comment on specific policies because of privacy concerns, he said. I asked if anybody could talk in general terms about limits on outpatient services.

Rob Guilbert, vice president of corporate communications, called and read a statement. "Assurant Health is committed to meeting the needs of our customers and complying with the provisions of their policies. As part of this goal, our company offers a variety of products and policy options to address the varying insurance needs of our customers."

A spokesperson for Blue Cross and Blue Shield of Missouri told me that Blue Cross does not offer policies with limitations on outpatient services.

While most attention in politics is focused on the millions of Americans with no health insurance, Dr. James Kimmey, chief executive of the nonprofit Missouri Foundation for Health, said the problem of people with inadequate health insurance is probably widespread as well.

"It's hard to get a number on them, though," Kimmey said. "People don't understand the health care system. They don't understand exclusions and limitations. We always talk about the people with no health insurance, but the underinsured are the nasty little secret in the health insurance system."

MAN WHO WASN'T REALLY HER FATHER MAY HAVE LEFT A LEGACY

10.17.2008

Judy Hall is retired from a long career as a secretary in the St. Louis public school system. Not long ago, one of her friends suggested she check the state's unclaimed property register. "I looked and found $3,000," said the friend.

So Judy checked. She went online to the Missouri treasurer's office and checked the unclaimed property register. Wow. There were two pieces of unclaimed property for her late father. The property could be almost anything. A bank account, an insurance policy, anything. Each had a value of "over $50." For some reason, $50 is the cutoff number. If you have unclaimed property worth $10,000, it is listed as "over $50."

The owner of these properties was Joseph Kelly. His address was in the 2300 block of University Street.

Judy remembered that address. Her father's mother was a live-in housekeeper at that address. Judy used to visit her grandmother there. Judy recalled an eccentric older man who employed her grandmother – Mr. McMahon. She remembered a windup Victrola in the living room.

You might think that once Judy had the good fortune to find the listings in the unclaimed property register that she could just claim the property.

Hardly.

"We were a dysfunctional family," Judy told me when I visited her home near Carondelet Park. "My mother was an alcoholic, and she and my father fought all the time." Eventually, her father, who was a good deal older than her mother, left the family. Judy thinks she was 18 when he left. Maybe 17. She didn't know where he went. Nor did she realize exactly how dysfunctional the family was.

When she was 19, she got married. She went to the Health Department to get a copy of her birth certificate. It listed her father as Harry Newton Goodman, age 38, occupation U.S. Navy. He was from Wolflake, Ill.

Judy had never heard of Harry Newton Goodman. Her earliest memories were of her father, Joseph James Kelly. She had been born in St. Louis in 1944. What was a guy from the Navy doing in St. Louis during the war?

It was all too much. Judy asked her mother what this was all about, but her mother refused to discuss it. Judy had no intention of looking into it. She did not feel like a Goodman. Nor did she feel like an Eckenfels, which was her mother's maiden name. She felt like a Kelly. All her school records had her as Kelly. Her baptism at St. Francis Xavier Church had her as Kelly. By the way, her baptism papers list her father as Joseph James Kelly. But she was 9 when she was baptized, so that proves nothing.

She went to court and had her name legally changed to Kelly. She was issued a new birth certificate.

Then, as Judy Kelly, she married William Hall and became Judy Hall. That was in 1963. They are still married. No dysfunctional marriage for them.

Shortly after Judy got married, she heard that her father had died in Texas. Exactly when or how was unclear. What did become clear was this: Her mother had never been married to Kelly. Judy learned that when her mother was unable to get Social Security death benefits for herself and Judy's younger sister.

Life moved along. Judy and her husband had two children. Judy's mother died. Her younger sister moved to Nevada. Judy gave little thought to the old days.

Then came this unclaimed property thing. The magic of found money.

"I can't imagine it's much," Judy said. "I remember the old life insurance policies. They might be for $200 or something. A man would come around weekly to collect 50 cents. That's probably what this is."

I am of a less practical bent. More of a dreamer. I asked if the house on University was large. Yes, it was, said Judy.

That got me to thinking. A rich, eccentric old man. His devoted housekeeper. Perhaps this property comes from him and through his housekeeper to her son. Why else would Kelly's address be on University? He didn't live there. His mother did. She has to figure into this mystery.

She is, of course, long gone. McMahon, too. For that matter, Joseph Kelly has been dead for nearly half a century. Judy figured that, too, might be a problem.

In order to collect the property, an heir must first produce a death certificate to prove that the original owner is deceased. Judy wondered if it would even be possible to find a death certificate for a Joseph Kelly who died somewhere in Texas sometime in the early '60s.

Not to worry. Matthew Fernandes, a news researcher here at the paper, checked Texas records and found that a Joseph James Kelly died in 1962 in Tarrant County. A death certificate would be no problem.

Still, only an heir can claim the property. Judy's claim is fragile. What about the younger sister who moved to Nevada? Who is listed as the father on her birth certificate? Joseph James Kelly.

"I was 9 when she was born so that explains that," Judy said. "I know this doesn't mean anything, but we look very much alike."

In addition to looking alike, I hope the sister is as easygoing as Judy. What if the property is really worth something? I called the treasurer's office to see if I could learn more about those two pieces of unclaimed property. No, said a supervisor.

Bill McClellan • Gently Down the Stream

LUTHERAN PASTORS ANSWER THE CALL

5.2.2010

The Rev. Glen Thomas had a devilish task in front of him. He was giving the sermon Tuesday evening at the Assignment of Calls service at Concordia Seminary.

This is a most drama-laden night for seminarians and their wives. It is the night they are called – assigned – to their first church. The Lutheran Church-Missouri Synod has churches in all 50 states and Canada. For reasons that perhaps only Lutherans understand, many of these churches are in very cold places.

The LCMS is split into 35 districts. There is a Minnesota North and a Minnesota South, a Wisconsin North and a Wisconsin South. Meanwhile, California shares a district with Nevada and Hawaii.

So as Thomas looked out at more than 100 anxious seminarians and their equally anxious wives, he understood that most of them, despite their appreciation of a good homily, just wanted to get on with the program. Where would they be going? How cold would it be?

Yet if Thomas were to glance to his left, he could see assembled the officials of the church, including the presidents of the 35 national districts. Stern-looking men, I thought. Men who have looked winter in the eye and not blinked. Some of them had traveled a long way for this, and they probably expected a full-fledged sermon.

Perhaps recalling his own anxiety when he wore a seminarian's robe in 1982 – he was called to Mascoutah – Thomas opted for brief. He spoke of the joy the seminarians would feel when they fed the flock the pure spiritual food of God's word, but he kept the sermon light by building it around the words of Yogi Berra: It isn't over until it's over.

Then the Rev. Gerald Kieschnick, president of the LCMS, rose from the ranks of the church officials. He looked stern, but was not. He acknowledged that seminarians on the cusp of Call pay scant attention to sermons. I can't recall who was in the pulpit or what he said at my Call, Kieschnick said. I think he talked about sin, and I think he was against it, he said.

By the way, Kieschnick was called in 1970 to Biloxi, Miss. His wife, Terry, told me that her mother-in-law had leaned over and said to her, "That's where the hurricanes come in."

Then it was time for this year's Call.

The Rev. Robert Hoehner did the honors. He is Concordia's director of placement. In March and then again in April, he gets together with church officials and the placement director of the other LCMS seminary, in Indiana, to fit the men to the churches. Actually, not just the men. Hoehner and his colleagues try to take into account the wives, too. Some have careers or educational opportunities that must be factored into the placements. But in the end, a pastor goes where the church needs him.

Hoehner understands that. He was hoping for a missionary position in Europe when he was called in 1972. Instead, he was called to Linn, Kan., a town of about 400. The church lacked indoor plumbing. In fact, church officials were thinking of closing the church. They did not, and last year, Hoehner placed a man at his old church.

By the way, there are two tracks. A man can go to a small church and be the pastor, or he can go to a larger church and be part of a team ministry. Churches that are looking for associate pastors are allowed to interview candidates.

The first call Tuesday night was to a church in Ohio. Then Texas. Then California, Michigan, Missouri, Minnesota, Wisconsin, Nebraska, Louisiana and Minnesota.

Next up was Stephen Carretto. I had spoken with him earlier. He and his wife, Jessica, were hoping for Florida. After a seminarian's second year of academics, he does a vicarage – sort of a pastoral internship – at a church for a year. Carretto had done his at a church in Boca Raton. "It was great," he said. But he had been interviewed by other churches, as well, and had no guarantee he'd go back to Florida.

Now it was his turn. He was called to Boca Raton.

Another man I had spoken with earlier was Todd McMurry. He's from St. Louis and was a firefighter before going to the seminary. He said he was on track to be a solo pastor. His wife, Kristin, is an optometrist. They were hoping for an urban area so she could more easily find work. Also, no place too cold.

Now it was his turn. He was called to Brooklyn, Minn.

That's a nice-sized city, and it's close to Minneapolis. Not exactly warm, but McMurry was smiling broadly as he shook hands with the officials, and I recalled what he had said earlier. "God will use us for his purposes."

That could have been the theme of the evening. There was an undercurrent of good-natured laughter when one man was called to Juneau, Alaska, and another to Fairbanks. But there was an overwhelming feeling of excitement and anticipation as a new batch of pastors prepared to enter the far-flung world.

"We'll miss all of you," said the Rev. Dale Meyer, the seminary president, who was called to Venedy, Ill., in 1973.

'INTERACTING' LETS
PASSIVE FOLKS BE AGGRESSIVE

2.20.2009

I received an e-mail the other morning about an incident in California in which a college student allegedly quoted the Bible during a discussion about same-sex marriages, and the professor allegedly cut him off and called him a name.

"Now that we're buddies, did you hear about this?" said the e-mailer. "This was sent to me earlier this morning. Maybe it's not true, but if it is, what do you think about it?"

The e-mailer and I are not buddies. We recently had what diplomats would call a "frank exchange of opinions," but it ended on a courteous note. I apologized for losing my temper. I do that sometimes. I lose patience with e-mailers, respond in kind to their notes and then apologize.

At any rate, I glanced at the story the e-mailer sent me. Who knows if it's true? The Internet is filled with garbage. I sent the e-mailer a note. "Why am I supposed to comment on that? If I do, then you're going to send me whatever goofy stuff you find? No thanks."

I wondered about the e-mailer. I do that sometimes, too. I wonder about people. For instance, I wonder about the aggressive drivers I see on my way to work. I'm usually in the right hand lane, putting along and somebody will come roaring in the passing lane and zoom up to a car, get right on its tail, swerve around it, and zoom up to the next car.

What does somebody like that do when he gets to work? Is he aggressive, quick to jump in a colleague's face? Or is he a quiet guy, the sort of person you wouldn't suspect of road rage?

What about the e-mailers? I get lots of e-mails. Some of it is partisan stuff, aggressive. Most of these e-mails are sent during working hours. What are these people like at work?

My "buddy" works at a company in Maryland Heights. The company's name and address are on his e-mail. Is he angry at work, always blasting Clinton and Obama and all other liberals, or is he quiet and seemingly respectful of other people's opinions?

Certainly, it's easier to be aggressive on a computer. The automatic social restraints of face-to-face discourse are absent with e-mails. Just as it's easier to be aggressive in a car. Or maybe the aggressive driver acts the same way in a crowd. Maybe as he leaves a ball game, he tries to push his way past people? I somehow doubt it.

But what I really wonder about with the e-mailers is productivity. I get most of these notes during normal working hours. It's unlikely that all these people work the night shift. For instance, my "buddy" is a sales rep. Assuming he works a day shift, he's on the clock when he's communicating with like-minded individuals – "This was sent to me earlier this morning" – and he's on the clock when he's challenging liberals like me to respond to this stuff.

And, of course, there's me. I do respond to this stuff – even if it's to insist that I'm not going to respond to this stuff – and I'm doing so while on the clock. There is an odd note to that, though. With the traditional newspaper business model sliding into the tank, people like me are supposed to respond to people. Being "interactive" is the way of the future.

Truth is, I do more harm than good when I interact. During the last election, I wrote a column in which I expressed my admiration for Sarah Palin. How come my side got stuck with Joe Biden, an old plagiarist? He was gracious when he got caught. He can take a good kicking. But still, why couldn't we have found somebody fresh and exciting like Sarah?

I got into a lot of "interactive" discussions about that. The one I remember most was with a man who also liked Sarah. He couldn't understand why I was supporting Obama. "I'm for McCain," he wrote. "I'm a veteran, and the number one thing to me is military experience. McCain has it. Obama doesn't."

I wrote back. "You supported John Kerry, did you?"

It turned out he most definitely did not support John Kerry. That kicked off a spirited interaction that ended with him announcing that he was going to cancel his subscription. I gave him the number for the circulation department.

I hadn't felt so good since we chased Bill Bidwill and his football team out of town.

What is all this interaction doing for society? Maybe it's good for democracy – we're communicating with each other. You think?

I sometimes read the comments that follow stories on the Internet version of this newspaper. Sometimes the comments are thoughtful and civil, but often they're not. Usually the writers have pen names. At first I found that puzzling, but then I figured it out.

They're doing all this interacting on company time. I imagine a comment poster. He drives aggressively to work, meekly says hello to the boss, sits down at his computer, reads the paper and then checks his e-mail to see if any of his like-minded buddies have sent him anything. Oh, good, they have! He fires an e-mail out to somebody like me. "What do you think of this, you liberal!" Then he goes back to reading the online news and prepares to engage others in a spirited discussion.

People in other cubicles in other businesses are doing the same thing. Some of them disagree with the first poster. "You're a moron!" one writes. "You're the moron!" somebody else fires back.

Meanwhile, American business sinks. I imagine the epitaph on its tombstone: Too much interaction. Not enough work.

YOUNG HISTORIAN SHED LIGHT ON VIETNAM

3.8.2009

Keith Nolan was 43 when he was diagnosed with lung cancer. He didn't smoke. Not regularly, anyway. He might have a cigarette now and then when he was drinking, but essentially, he was a nonsmoker. The doctors told him the cancer was probably genetic. His father had survived throat cancer and tongue cancer.

Nolan was living in the basement of his father's house when I visited him in January 2008. "The doctors say I have a year left," Nolan told me. The doctors were off by about a month. Nolan died Feb. 19.

I liked Nolan a lot, and I very much admired his work. He was a historian. He wrote nonfiction books about the Vietnam War.

He was, of course, far too young to have served in that war. He was 3 years old when the North Vietnamese overran Hue during the Tet Offensive of 1968. The battle to retake that city was the subject of his first book, which he wrote when he was in high school. It was a remarkable effort for a high school kid. He used after-action reports and interviewed veterans of the battle. Still, that first book was the work of a young man with an agenda. He intended to show that the war was a more noble cause than people thought.

His later books became more realistic. "Combat with all the warts," said retired Marine Corps Lt. Col. Gary Solis. Military publications gave his books rave reviews. Historian Stephen Ambrose praised his work. So did the men who fought the sometimes obscure battles of which he wrote.

Even so, these were always niche books. The market for nonfiction about the Vietnam War was limited. Nolan made a living, but he didn't get rich. He never made enough to visit Vietnam.

When I visited him a year ago, he told me he was working on a final, big book. His most ambitious project. He was going to follow an Air Cav unit from the time it arrived in Vietnam to the time it left. He said he thought the book would show how the war evolved, and how the morale shifted. It was going to provide a more comprehensive picture of the war than any of his previous books. He had begun reading after-action reports and had begun conducting interviews. But he never finished.

A memorial Mass was celebrated for him last Saturday at St. Joachim Church in Old Mines, not too far from the place in Washington County where he and his ex-wife, Kelly, had tried to make a home.

I had met Kelly once before. She seems nice. Marriages can be as complicated and nuanced as history. I had also met their daughter Britt. She seems like a terrific kid.

But most of the people in the church were strangers to me, and as I looked around, I wondered which ones were veterans who had come to pay their respects to the man who had chronicled their long-ago battles. An older man sitting across the aisle from me had the bearing of an officer. Maybe he was a captain or a major 40 years ago. Maybe Nolan had written about the most desperate days of the man's life.

I looked around the church at other people who might be veterans. This is another ending, I thought, like the last helicopter leaving the roof of the embassy. The best historian of the Vietnam War has died, and his death comes just as his own generation takes over, and the boomers, who have been obsessed with Vietnam for 40 years, yield the political stage.

It seems fitting. The country has new wars and new veterans with which to concern itself.

Maybe it's time we can take stock. One of the nice things about Nolan's books was that he usually included an appendix in which he briefly mentioned what the various veterans had done when they left the service. Mostly, they took ordinary jobs. This one became a lineman for a utility company, and that one went back to college and became a high school teacher and wrestling coach. Middle managers, cops, lawyers, small-businessmen. Most got married. In other words, they got on with life.

It's interesting, I suppose, that no Vietnam veteran became president. Sixteen years of boomers in the White House. One opposed the war and was a protester, the other supported the war but avoided it by getting into a National Guard unit. Both surrounded themselves mostly with like-minded people.

After the Mass, we gathered for lunch at the St. Michael House off Highway CC. I introduced myself to the man who had been sitting across the aisle from me. Paul Knese said he had not been in any of the books. He is a financial planner and a friend of the family's. I thought you were an officer, I said. I was, he said. I was a pilot over there, he said.

I met George Murphy and his wife, Mary. They had come in from Newark, Ill. Murphy served with the 101st Airborne at Firebase Ripcord in the A Shau Valley in April 1970. The four-month battle for the firebase – a battle the U.S. lost – was the subject of Nolan's book, "Ripcord."

On the inside cover is a quote from the Marine Corps Gazette. "Readers should not be surprised if this battle is unknown to them. Astonishingly, it went virtually unreported by the media at the time, largely because of the close wraps imposed by the Military Assistance Command Vietnam headquarters in Saigon. … It was an unknown battle until Keith Nolan rightly decided that this is a story that had to be told. Military professionals and historians alike will be gratified that Mr. Nolan made that decision."

Murphy told me the veterans of Ripcord have formed an association based on the book. "The government tried to keep this quiet," he said. "And they did until Nolan came along."

That was, I thought, a wonderful epitaph for a historian.

YOU TALKING TO ME?
THEN PLEASE QUIT WHISPERING

2.13.2008

The weather Tuesday was cold and dreary, and the mail was worse. The first thing I saw was an official-looking envelope from the Southwestern Hearing Center. On the outside of the envelope was written: "HEALTH NOTIFICATION BULLETIN. OFFICIAL AND DATED MATERIAL. OPEN IMMEDIATELY."

I opened it. It was a check! The check was for $1,013.56. Was this a mistake? No, apparently not. It was clearly a check from the Southwestern Hearing Center and it was made out to me. It was endorsed by Michael Marino, CEO. Then I noticed something written in light blue ink at the bottom of the check. "This is not a check," it said.

Instead, it turned out to be a coupon worth up to $1,013.56 if I were to "upgrade" to a set of Rhapsody Elite hearing instruments.

Sadly, I need a hearing aid. I've even been to an audiologist. He gave me a series of tests. "You need a hearing aid," he finally said. "What?" I responded.

Actually, I'm onto the tricks of that particular trade. Everybody in that business is trained to speak softly. The audiologist himself was practically whispering. I made a scene. "I know exactly what you're doing. I wasn't born yesterday," I shouted. "That's why you need a hearing aid," the audiologist whispered back. So I stormed out.

Apparently, he sold my name to people in the industry.

That's fine with me. I need a hearing aid, and I can surely use a coupon worth up to $1,013.56. One of the oddities of the health insurance system is that most health plans do not cover hearing aids. That's ridiculous. People routinely abuse the system and demand tests they don't need, but nobody who doesn't need a hearing aid tries to get one.

The lack of coverage is especially ludicrous in the newspaper business. I'm a reporter. I depend on hearing people. Lately, that has become difficult. Sometimes I get angry calls. "I've had it with you, McClellan! You misquoted me." "Pardon me?" "I said you misquoted me!" "If you don't stop whispering, I'm going to hang up right now." And then I do.

But this hearing loss is part of getting older, and I'm trying to age gracefully. I decided to call the number in the letter that came with the check. It was an 800 number. The woman who answered said she would give my name to the people at the local office. "What is your name?" she whispered. "Bill McClellan," I said. "Can you spell that?" she asked.

At that point, I lost my temper.

"Of course I can spell my own name!" I shouted. "I'm losing my hearing, but my mind is still perfectly sharp!"

After I hung up on her, I went back to the rest of the mail. There was a letter from the Neptune Society. On the outside of the envelope was written: "Free Pre-Paid Cremation! Details inside."

Who sold my name to these people?

I remembered that I had a routine physical exam just a couple of weeks ago.

Routine? At least I thought so. Maybe my doctor looked at the results and immediately sold my name to the Neptune Society.

With some trepidation, I opened the envelope. "Simple, Economical and Dignified. That's our motto! With everyone moving around these days, placing a loved one in a 'local' cemetery may not be as functional as it used to be."

That seemed to be rather generic, and that was good news. At the bottom of the letter was even better news. "Please accept our apologies if this letter has reached you at a time of serious illness."

Well, all right! They don't know anything about me. This is a random sort of letter. The Neptune Society probably buys the same list the hearing aid people buy. Mature adults.

My wife was suddenly at my shoulder. I had not even heard her approach. "Neptune Society?" she asked.

"You'd think they'd bury people at sea, which doesn't sound so bad, but they don't. They cremate them," I explained. "I'm eligible for a free cremation."

She seemed to think about that for a minute. "They probably just want to sell you an expensive urn," she said. Or something like that. The way she whispers these days, it's hard to know exactly what she says.

NAME GAME NEARLY BACKFIRES ON MAN HELD ON FORGERY CHARGE

12.24.2006

'Twas the last working day before Christmas, and all through the courthouse defendants hoped for a break, none more so than Willie Davis.

He had been locked up at the City Workhouse since the middle of September, and on Friday morning he was hoping Judge Elizabeth Hogan would set him free. Giving some credence to his hope was this: Everybody knew he was innocent.

Sort of innocent. Davis had been locked up on a forgery charge that was committed, according to the state, by Lonzell Harts. The problem Davis had was that Lonzell Harts is one of his many aliases. He's been Kevin McCoy, Melvin Steele, Angelo Garrett, Charles Brooks and so on and so forth.

Aliases, of course, are used when a fellow does not want the police to know his true identity. Maybe there is a warrant out for his arrest. Maybe he is on probation or parole. The downside of using somebody else's name is that the person whose name you're borrowing may have a warrant out for his arrest.

Perhaps that is what happened in September. For reasons that remain a little fuzzy, Davis was arrested in September and charged with Harts' forgery.

Fortunately, Davis had a great alibi. He had been in jail when Harts – or somebody using Harts' name – had committed the forgery.

But how do you get that word out?

The public defender's office represents a lot of people, and a good number of them claim to be innocent. It's hard to put one person's claim in front of somebody else's claim, so generally, a person has to wait until it's his turn to go to trial.

Furthermore, Davis is not the sort of fellow whose word is going to carry much weight. As befits a 54-year-old man who has used 16 names, three Social Security numbers and several birth dates over the years, he has been in and out of trouble for most of his adult life. A bunch of arrests and a couple of stretches in prison. The most positive thing you can say about his record is that almost all of it has to do with possessing controlled substances of one sort or another. Had he been born with money, perhaps he'd have a medical problem instead of a criminal record.

And so he sat in the workhouse. Finally, after a letter-writing campaign, somebody checked his fingerprints with the fingerprints of the man who originally had been arrested for the forgery. They were different.

Only a misdemeanor warrant stood between Davis and freedom. He had been charged with second-degree property damage after allegedly throwing a brick through somebody's windshield. Because he had done more than three months on the forgery charge, the solution seemed simple. A 90-day sentence for the property damage, and with credit for time served, Davis would be out for Christmas.

He was part of the "confined docket" in Division 26. There were about two dozen of them, and they came clanking into the courtroom, shackled together in groups of six like the Ghosts of a very sad Christmas Present. Most were wearing rumpled civilian clothes. They had been arrested the night before. A few of them, like Davis, had been guests of the city for a while longer and wore orange jumpsuits.

Most of the one-nighters had been arrested for traffic charges. Driving with a revoked license seemed common. Some asked for trial dates, some pleaded guilty and were given probation.

Finally, it was Davis' turn. He pleaded guilty to property damage and was given time served. Then the judge studied some papers and asked Davis if he hadn't pleaded guilty to some kind of drug charge just a while ago? Was this a probation violation?

No, said Davis. That wasn't me.

For an instant, I thought that somebody had borrowed his name – maybe Lonzell Harts – and the whole deal would come undone. But no, that was a different Willie Davis. At least we think it was. Davis was ordered released.

FROM CUBA, WITH LOVE: NO DICTATING WHAT HEART KNOWS

3.2.2008

Maria Flores and Orlando Recio were married 62 years ago in Havana, Cuba. In the wedding photo, Maria looks radiant in her white dress. Orlando is movie-star handsome in his police uniform. He and his bride are walking under a canopy of swords held by fellow officers.

Maria had grown up in Santiago, a city in southwest Cuba. Her father, Pedro, was a self-made man. He had come from a poor farming family. As a young man, he carted produce into the city to sell. He saved his money. He sent his three children to college. Maria became a lawyer. She was about 30 when she met Orlando at a party. She saw him across the room. How could she not? At 6-foot-4, he stood out in a crowd. He spotted her, too, and soon they were talking, laughing. From that first moment, she knew they would marry.

They began dating, but in the traditional way – that is, with a chaperon. Usually, Maria's younger brother filled the role.

Maria and Orlando were married in March 1946. Sixteen months later, they had a daughter, Adelina.

The family moved to Santiago, and Orlando worked for his father-in-law. By this time, Pedro Flores was a successful businessman. For the most part, Maria stayed home and cared for her daughter. In the 1950s, there were rebels in the mountains, but the idea of revolution seemed far away. Maria took a case in which she represented a man who was accused of having ties to the rebel leader, Fidel Castro. Mostly, though, their lives seemed unaffected by politics.

Castro toppled the government in 1959. Pedro Flores was arrested and sentenced to prison on trumped-up charges. Orlando knew somebody in the new government, and Flores was released. Still, it was a chilling event.

In November 1960, Maria and Orlando sent their daughter to live with relatives in Miami. In July 1961, they joined her.

In those days, Cubans were allowed to leave the country, but they were allowed to take only some clothes and one box of cigars. Before granting permission to leave, the government would send someone to the house to take inventory. No one was supposed to take wealth out of the country.

Maria and Orlando arrived in Miami with virtually nothing. They were starting over in their early 40s. They stayed with relatives. Orlando got a job at a hotel. He parked cars. Maria became a baby sitter. While taking English classes, she heard that Indiana State University was sending representatives to Miami to interview Cuban professionals and would be offering scholarships to some of them. Maria interviewed and was offered a scholarship. The family moved to Terre Haute. There was an opening in the program, and Orlando was accepted. They began studying to become teachers.

So Orlando and Maria became high school Spanish teachers. Maria got a job at Webster Groves. The family moved here. Orlando got a job teaching Spanish to Peace Corps volunteers, and then he got a job at Kirkwood High School.

The years went by. They became U.S. citizens, and proud citizens, too. But still, they sometimes talked wistfully of returning to Cuba.

In some ways, they were still the couple in the wedding photo. Orlando was a dashing figure, the sort of man who went to a party and was soon surrounded by people. Maria was quiet. But she ran things, said their daughter, Adelina. "She was the brains of the operation, but she made the decisions in such a way that he thought he was making them with her. They complemented each other so well. She was always blindly in love with him, and he relied on her completely."

When Orlando was in his 60s, his health began to fail. First, it was arthritis; then, a form of Parkinson's.

"It was sad to watch," said Adelina. "This tall guy, always so strong, and his body was failing him. She did everything for him."

Two months ago, Orlando, who got around with the aid of a walker, fell in their home. Maria could not get him up. She called 911. The paramedics told Orlando they were going to take him to the hospital. He refused to go. Maria leaned over and wagged her finger at him. "You will," she said. "All right," he said.

Doctors determined he had fractured two vertebrae in his neck. He was sent to St. Luke Hospital's Surrey Place to rehab.

Shortly before Valentine's Day, Maria fell and broke her hip. She was taken to Missouri Baptist Hospital. She had surgery. She came out of that surgery fine, and the plan was to reunite the couple at Surrey Place.

They were frantic being apart. Adelina was running from one hospital to the other, assuring each that the other was fine. Then on Thursday night, Valentine's Day, Maria seemed to weaken. Adelina left her and went to see Orlando. He seemed fine, but in the early morning hours that Friday, Adelina got a call. Her father had died. Adelina could not bear to tell her mother. In the morning when she visited her mother, Maria asked, "How is he?" "I just saw him," said Adelina casually. In the early morning hours Saturday, Maria died.

She died without knowing Orlando had died. Or did she? A doctor said to Adelina, "He must have put in a spiritual call to her."

Three days later, Fidel Castro announced his resignation.

MURDER MAY BE KEY TO DRUG DEALER'S CELL

1.31.2010 • First of two columns

On a summer morning in 1983, Alan Milburn, who was then 34 years old, appeared in federal court in St. Louis to be sentenced on drug charges. He had been convicted of running a marijuana and cocaine ring in Cape Girardeau. He had been charged under the Continuing Criminal Enterprise statute, which required a minimum sentence of 10 years.

Judge William Hungate, folksy and unpredictable, looked down from the bench and asked Milburn if he had anything to say.

"No, your Honor," said Milburn. "Nothing?" the judge asked. "No, sir."

Hungate then pronounced sentence: life in prison without the possibility of parole.

Even the two assistant U.S. attorneys who had prosecuted the case, Mitch Stevens and Jim Crowe, were surprised at the severity of the sentence. Milburn was stunned. He was taken to a hold-over cell, where he broke down and cried.

Twelve years earlier, fresh out of Southeast Missouri State with a degree in education, he had been hired as an English teacher at Sikeston High School, the high school from which he had graduated.

He was a popular teacher – young, handsome, athletic and cool. Maybe too cool. As he prepared to begin his third year of teaching, the superintendent asked about rumors that Milburn smoked pot. Milburn admitted he did. He was asked to resign. He did.

In his early, casual days of pot smoking, Milburn would sometimes buy 4 ounces of pot, sell 3 of them and make just enough profit to cover his own ounce. After he left his teaching job, the ounces became pounds. Lots and lots of them.

In 1974, he was arrested at Lambert airport when he tried to pick up a package containing 135 pounds of pot. He received probation but the next year was stopped for speeding in Arkansas. He had 9 pounds of pot and $10,000 in cash in the car.

Actually, the 9 pounds was nothing. He and several associates were bringing in 300-pound loads of Mexican pot from Texas and similar loads of Colombian pot from Florida.

He eventually went to jail for the Arkansas case. While he was locked up – he did about 18 months – his girlfriend, Debbie Martin, helped run the drug business.

He had met Debbie while teaching in Sikeston. She had been a student at the high school but not in his class. She was a doctor's daughter. She graduated in the spring of 1973 and headed to Cape Girardeau for college. When Milburn resigned that summer, he headed to Cape, too. Soon they were living together.

Shortly after Milburn returned from Arkansas, the drug business evolved from pot to cocaine. Also, Milburn and Martin opened an antique and plant shop called Mother Earth. It was across the street from the federal courthouse.

In September 1979, Milburn drove to Texas to buy antiques and cocaine. While he was gone, Martin was murdered. Her body was found at the bottom of a stairway in the building that contained the antique shop.

Police questioned Milburn, but he had proof he had been in Dallas. Suspicion turned to Max Ellison, a former Stoddard County deputy sheriff whose younger brother had once dated Martin. Two friends of Martin's told police that she had said she was meeting Ellison that weekend, and that he wanted to borrow money for some kind of plan involving guns or drugs.

Shortly after Martin's murder, Ellison went to a bank to purchase certificates of deposit. He had $80,000 in cash. That all seemed highly suspicious, but it was not enough for an arrest.

A couple of weeks after the murder, Milburn checked a safe he kept at his sister's house. The last time he had checked, there was $93,000 in it. Now the safe was empty. He figured the missing money had to be connected to Debbie's death, but how can a drug dealer go to police and tell them he is missing $93,000 in cash? He said nothing.

Within a couple of years, Milburn's drug ring began to unravel. A longtime associate agreed to wear a wire. The feds began amassing evidence.

In August 1982, Milburn and 11 others were indicted. There were two parallel tracks – money laundering and tax evasion, and the drug charges. As to the latter, the government alleged that Milburn and his associates had distributed about 35 pounds of cocaine. In his appeals, Milburn argued the number of pounds was about a third of that.

Either way, it was a lot. Milburn may have been the largest drug dealer in southeast Missouri.

But life without the possibility of parole? Although Hungate, who died in June 2007, never felt the need to explain his sentence, some observers thought Martin's death may have been a factor.

"No one thought he killed her," Crowe said last week, "but he certainly led her into the life that brought her to that."

What nobody could guess is that 27 years later, her murder would lead to his release.

Next: A deal to testify, and a chance for freedom.

A DEAL IS STRUCK, THEN DEATH THROWS A CURVE

2.1.2010 • Second of two columns

Alan Milburn was sentenced to life without the possibility of parole for drug trafficking in 1983. He ran a major marijuana and cocaine ring in Cape Girardeau, but even the U.S. attorneys who prosecuted the case were surprised at the severity of the sentence.

Milburn appealed, but the appeals were denied. The sentence by a federal judge was severe but constitutional, said the appellate court. Milburn's fate was sealed.

Then, a couple of years ago, Detective Jimmy Smith of the Cape Girardeau Police Department was looking over the file of the 1979 murder of Debbie Martin.

Max Ellison, the chief suspect in the killing, had bought certificates of deposit with $80,000 in cash shortly after the murder. That money had to come from somewhere. Smith realized that Martin's boyfriend, Milburn, was a major drug dealer at the time.

Milburn had been in prison for nearly 25 years by the time Smith looked at the case, but perhaps Milburn could tie the $80,000 to Martin. Smith contacted one of Milburn's relatives. Could he help? Would he?

Milburn was then in Big Sandy federal prison in eastern Kentucky. That is a high security prison. The gangs there are powerful. If Milburn were to talk to any authorities, he'd be killed.

He requested a transfer to the medium-security federal prison in Marion, Ill. He was transferred in April 2008. Although it is still a risky place to be labeled a snitch, he agreed to talk with Smith. The two men knew each other slightly from years ago, when they were both tae kwon do instructors in Cape Girardeau.

Milburn told Smith that shortly after Martin's murder, he had discovered that

$93,000 in drug money was missing from his safe.

Smith returned to the prison with Cape Girardeau prosecutor Morley Swingle, who told Milburn that if he agreed to help in the case, Swingle would talk with the feds about a motion to reduce his sentence. Milburn agreed to testify against Ellison.

Swingle went to the U.S. attorney's office. Then-U.S. Attorney Catherine Hanaway and several high-ranking members of the office, including Jim Crowe, who now heads the criminal division and had been one of the prosecutors in Milburn's trial, discussed the matter.

"Swingle is a highly respected prosecutor, and we decided that if he felt this was important for a murder case, we'd go along," Crowe said.

Milburn's family contacted attorney Ron Jenkins, who had represented some of the family members when they were charged with tax evasion in connection with Milburn's drug ring. "This case has always stuck in my craw because I thought the sentence was so disproportionate," Jenkins said.

In May of last year, Milburn testified at Ellison's preliminary hearing. He talked about the missing money. He said the money had been in a safe to which only two people knew the combination – he and Debbie Martin.

"It was a dramatic moment," said Swingle. "Before he took the stand, he stood in front of the defense table and just stared at Ellison. Then he gave a slight smile."

The judge found probable cause and bound Ellison over for trial.

By the way, Ellison had been behind bars from 1985 to 2007 for kidnapping and armed robbery.

After he testified, Milburn went back to Marion to await Ellison's trial. One day an inmate handed him a story from the Cape Girardeau newspaper about the preliminary hearing. Milburn was exposed as a snitch.

"I told him, 'That guy murdered my girlfriend and stole my drug money, and I'm doing all I can to get him,'" Milburn recalled. "He said, 'By God, I'd do the same thing.'"

So all that was left was the trial. Then, perhaps freedom. The trial was set for March of this year.

In August of last year, Ellison died of a liver disease.

Milburn heard the news and figured his deal was off. He would die in prison.

"We had nothing in writing," Jenkins said. "But I told him these are honorable people. Jim Crowe and Catherine Hanaway and Morley Swingle are all people of their word."

But to Milburn, things seemed to be dragging on. The summer turned into the fall and then the winter.

Finally, on Jan. 21, the matter went to the federal courthouse in Cape Girardeau. The judge was Stephen Limbaugh Jr. He had been an assistant prosecutor in Cape Girardeau in 1979 and had been called to the murder scene.

Swingle spoke and told Limbaugh that he could not have brought a case against Ellison without Milburn's testimony, and that testimony had put Milburn at risk in prison. Crowe spoke, too: "When a person cooperates in significant cases, they are rewarded for that."

Limbaugh reduced Milburn's sentence to 40 years. With credit for the 27 years he had served, he was immediately eligible for parole. He was granted parole and released the next day, Jan. 22.

I spoke with Milburn, now 62, a couple of days later.

I asked if he had known Ellison. They played football together in high school but weren't buddies, he said. He added that he would have testified against Ellison even if he had not gotten a deal. "Frankly, I wanted him tarred and feathered and sent to the electric chair. Also, it was exoneration for me. A lot of people probably always thought I killed Debbie."

I asked if he had been worried the deal would fall through after Ellison's death. "Sure," he said. "But my God, Mr. Jim Crowe stood by his word."

What is Milburn going to do now?

"That's a good question. My feet haven't touched the ground yet."

PRACTICAL? NO, BUT CAT AND BOY MAKE A CHRISTMAS CONNECTION

12.24.2008

In the second week of December, a woman who volunteers at the Humane Society wrote me about a cat named Fiona.

She said Fiona came into the Humane Society in July. The woman did not know the circumstances that brought her there, but Fiona seemed intelligent, friendly and just so darned nice that the adoption counselors would bring her out of her cage to let people see how sweet a cat can be. Fiona would charm the people, and then they would select a kitten. "A lucky, clueless kitten," is the way the woman put it. And Fiona would be put back into her cage.

One day, Fiona gave up. She didn't move to the front of the cage when the counselors came. A Girl Scout troop visited, and the volunteers got Fiona out of her cage. "She lay curled in a ball and only raised her head once or twice," the woman said.

The woman was concerned. "There are only three reasons for the Humane Society to euthanize," she said. "If the animal is aggressive, if it is terminally ill or if it becomes depressed and just can't live in that damn cage anymore."

Like most volunteers, the woman had no room for more pets herself. Neither do I. The woman talked to her neighbors. No luck.

Or so we thought. Actually, Fiona's luck had already changed.

On Thanksgiving weekend, a cat named Cannonball developed a swollen lip. Cannonball is one of those animals born under a lucky star. His mother was a feral cat. Fortunately for Cannonball and his siblings, she had her litter in the window well of a home in Belleville. The homeowner, Joan Gettys, decided that all of those kittens would be adopted. She called her daughter, Jennifer Whinery, and Jennifer and her husband, Norm, agreed to take two of them. So Cannonball and a sibling, Lucy, joined the Whinery family in south St. Louis County. This was about five years ago.

When Cannonball developed his swollen lip on Thanksgiving weekend, Jennifer called her veterinarian. The office was closed for the holidays.

Jennifer decided to take Cannonball to the clinic at the Humane Society. Her 10-year-old son, Cameron, went with her. While Jennifer and Cannonball saw the vet, Cameron wandered around the cages. He saw Fiona. She is a white cat with black markings. They looked at each other. He put his finger in her cage and stroked her.

When he got home, he went on the computer and found the website for the Humane Society. He found Fiona's picture. He printed it out. He went to the wall where he had hung his Christmas list. An iPod and speakers were what he wanted. He took the list down and replaced it with Fiona's picture.

But his parents were not enthusiastic. Norm had been laid off from his job as a sales rep for a building supply company in late September. It didn't seem like a good time to take on another animal.

Sometimes you have to be practical.

They stayed firm until they saw Jennifer's brother and his wife, Jan, at a party. Jan is involved in an organization called Four Hearts Foundation, which works with the Belleville Humane Society. Jan is not a person who would vote for practicality in this kind of a situation. "Cameron has made a connection with that cat," she said. Knowing that times were tough for the Whinerys, she gave them a check to cover the adoption.

And so it was that the day after the volunteer had written me a note about the seemingly luckless Fiona, Norm visited the Humane Society to fill out the forms and make arrangements for the adoption.

He was taken back to see Fiona. She was lying down. Other cats came to the edge of their cages to vie for attention, but Fiona did not. Norm put his finger in the cage. No response. He thought it was odd, but this was the cat Cameron wanted, so this was the cat Norm was going to get.

The next night, the Whinerys pretended they had to talk to the vet at the Humane Society. In reality, they had printed a sign that was put on Fiona's cage: "I am going home with Cameron."

And she did. The Humane Society said she should be kept apart from the other cats for 10 days in case she had a disease. The Whinerys put her in the bathroom. Cameron moved his stuff in there and slept in the tub.

I visited the Whinerys on Tuesday. The 10 days is past, and Fiona has the run of the house. She has come back to life. She seems to tolerate Cannonball and Lucy, and they her, and she seems to like Cameron's sister, Emily, who is 6, but there is little doubt whose cat she is. She's Cameron's cat, and the only question is which one of them got the better gift this Christmas.

Bill McClellan • Gently Down the Stream

INSTITUTION TO HOME, TO GRAVE: OTTO, RIP

1.12.2007

Otto Richter was buried Thursday morning. There were a few relatives at the cemetery, some of whom had not seen Otto in many years. John Stahr, a funeral director at Jay B. Smith Funeral Homes, read a poem: "When I come to the end of the road and the sun has set for me, I want no rites in a gloom-filled room. Why cry for a soul set free?"

Charlene Wozniak was one of the mourners. She was Otto's niece. She used to visit him at the State Hospital on Arsenal when she was a child. She used to visit with her aunt, Henrietta. Charlene remembers Henrietta knocking on a door and a small window opening, and then a voice asking who they wanted to see. She remembers going into a large room. Uncle Otto sat at a table. He never had much to say.

When Charlene grew older, she asked her mother, Lucille, about Otto. Her mother said she did not want to discuss it. Much later, Henrietta told Charlene this story: When Otto was 16, he and two friends made a batch of alcohol. This sort of thing had been common during Prohibition. The alcohol was bad. One of the boys went blind. One had kidney failure. Then there was Otto. The bad alcohol damaged his mind. The family was unable to take care of him and he was institutionalized.

It is hard to verify this story. Otto was born in 1919, which means he would have been 16 in 1935. Prohibition had ended two years earlier. Of course, it's possible that people, especially teenage boys, would still be making their own booze.

Charlene has something of a file on her uncle. Among the papers is a letter from a clinical caseworker at the State Hospital. It was written in May 1967.

"The doctor considers that Mr. Richter no longer needs psychiatric care, but does need the supervision a nursing home will provide." So Otto was released to a nursing home. The letter said the cost of his care in the nursing home would be covered by a monthly pension fund from the welfare office. In addition to the care, Otto would receive $5 a month spending money.

That letter, incidentally, was written to Henrietta. She seems to have been devoted to her brother. She visited him every Sunday – both when he was in the State Hospital and during his years in nursing homes. According to Charlene, Henrietta didn't go on vacations, or if she did, she was always back by Sunday. She kept that schedule until her health deteriorated. She died two years ago at the age of 90. She never married. She worked as a clerk for the Internal Revenue Service.

Henrietta was the oldest of the six Richter children. Otto was the third oldest, behind Lucille, Charlene's mother.

Charlene, who married and had four children, was also a steady visitor during her uncle's years in various nursing homes. She said he seldom talked, and when he did, often only Henrietta could understand him.

According to the papers Charlene inherited from Henrietta, Otto had been temporarily returned to the State Hospital – Ward 5 of the Missouri Institute of Psychiatry – in 1973.

I called the hospital to see if I could find out when he was discharged to another nursing home, and, more importantly, when he was first admitted. All records are confidential, a supervisor told me. I asked if a family member could get the information. Even a family member would need a court order, the supervisor said.

So much for that. Secrets carried to the grave.

"A soul set free." I like that. I asked Stahr the name of the poem. I don't know, he said. Which seems appropriate for the poem that marked the end of the worldly journey of Otto Richter.

WHAT'S 2 WEEKS IN THE COUNTY JAIL TO A FELLOW WHO IS LUCKY IN LOVE?

5.6.2007

Friday morning was wet and dreary, and the St. Charles County jail is hardly a cheery place even on a sunny day, but Greg Roeder looked positively beatific as he sat on a bench in the third-floor waiting room. My first thought was that he was one of those perverse types who enjoy watching somebody else having a bad time. I was the somebody else.

I was at the jail to see David White. He is facing two counts of possession of a controlled substance. He is a persistent and prior offender, so he is facing some serious time. He was supposed to have had a preliminary hearing Friday morning, but when I checked the docket posted outside the courtroom, I didn't see his name. A woman from the prosecutor's office checked with the judge. "He'll have to be rescheduled," she said. "The judge has recused himself." I asked why. She shrugged.

When I realized White wouldn't be in court, I went over to the jail. Maybe I'd be able to see him. I took the elevator to the third-floor waiting room. I asked the deputy if I could see White. I'm not on his visiting list, I said.

Are you a lawyer?

No, a newspaper reporter.

The deputy left to consult with a higher authority. He came back in a couple of minutes. You need permission from Capt. Myers, he said. "Fine. Can I speak with the captain?" He's not in today, said the deputy. "Does anybody fill in for the captain when he's not here?" The deputy said something to the effect that he didn't think it would do any good, but he'd ask. He left.

I looked around. There was one other person in the waiting room. He seemed to be smiling.

The deputy came back. He said the captain would be back on Monday. I could try again then. The deputy left the waiting room, and I headed to the elevator. The smiling man spoke. Crazy place, he said, or something to that effect.

"Are you waiting to see somebody?" I asked.

Oh no, he said. I owe them two weeks, and I've taken some time off work. I'm going to spend my vacation here.

He told me he was 37 years old. He said he was getting his life in order, and after he gave the county these two weeks, he would be free and clear. Most importantly, he was back with his first wife, the woman he has always loved.

As regular readers know, I have a soft spot for love stories. I pulled out my notebook and sat down.

He said that he and Bonnie had gone to high school together, but she had not been attracted to him. "She thought I was a dork." When they were both 21, they met again, at the Dirty Duck bar in St. Peters. They were married in May 1994. They had two children, but then the marriage went bad. It was all his fault, Roeder said. Drinking, running around, that sort of stuff.

After the divorce, Roeder continued on his downward spiral. He fell behind in child support payments. The state suspended his drivers license. "I didn't even know," he said.

He and Bonnie both remarried and then divorced. Perhaps when there is one person in the world for you, that is to be expected.

One night he was pulled over and then arrested for driving on a suspended license. It was that sort of minor trouble, he said, that led to him owing the county a couple of weeks.

But none of that mattered because he and his wife had gotten back together. He said that his own folks had gotten divorced and then remarried. That is exactly what he has in mind, he said. He added that he'd love to get remarried on his anniversary, but he was still going to be in jail. Nevertheless, this trip to jail was redemptive in nature, a second beginning.

Suddenly, the deputy reappeared. He explained that I did not have permission to talk with Roeder, who was, more or less, already in custody. But he wasn't yet locked up, I argued. Doesn't matter, said the deputy.

No problem, I said. I left feeling pretty good. Roeder's good spirits had lifted my own. Besides, it's an ungrateful man who complains about getting kicked out of jail.

LOTS OF HISTORY IN ONE LITTLE HOUSE

7.12.2009

Sometime around 1850, a small group of Huguenots – Protestants who fled France to avoid religious persecution – came up the Mississippi River from New Orleans and settled in the Illinois farm country near Highland, in a village called Sebastopol.

Jocelyn Ulmet was born there in May 1911. Shortly thereafter, her family moved about 20 miles northwest to a farm near Greenville.

The family then attended the Smith Grove Baptist Church. The patriarch of the Smith family had served in the British military during the Revolutionary War. Whether he deserted or waited until after the war to switch sides is unclear. All we know is that his descendants arrived in the Greenville area around 1820.

Kenneth R. Smith was born in January 1911, and he met Jocelyn Ulmet at the church named for his family.

The two youngsters attended different one-room grade schools, but both attended Greenville High School. They graduated in 1928.

Jocelyn completed a secretarial course at Greenville College. Kenneth headed to St. Louis to seek his fortune. He intended to become a lawyer. But the Great Depression interfered with those plans. He got an office job with the railroad and then returned to Illinois. He rented 60 acres to farm and married Jocelyn in 1932.

By that time, she was working as a secretary for the Greenville school district. Married women were not allowed to work for the school district, so Jocelyn and Kenneth were married quietly by a justice of the peace in East St. Louis.

A year later, the first of their six children was born, and Jocelyn's secretarial career was finished. By 1938, there were three kids. A drought and low prices made farm life difficult. Kenneth got a job as a rural mail carrier. In 1939, the family built a house in Greenville.

It was a Sears house. A house from a kit. Thousands of pieces – lumber, nails, light fixtures, blueprints, everything – arrived by train. A horse and wagon carried the material to the site on Eastern Avenue.

Jocelyn's father and uncle, both carpenters, helped Kenneth. They used a team of horses to dig out the basement, which featured a coal bin and a furnace. The first floor had a kitchen, a living room, a small breakfast nook, a dining room and a half bath. The second floor had four small bedrooms and a full bath.

Kenneth, Jocelyn and the three kids moved in. Before long, there were three more kids. When the weather was good and the roads were clear, Kenneth could finish his mail route in about four hours. So he bought some land out of town and he farmed. Also, the family had a large garden. Jocelyn canned vegetables and churned butter. More often than not, meat came from a relative's farm.

The years passed.

The oldest son became a neurosurgeon. The next became a businessman. The oldest daughter became a nurse. The next daughter became a school teacher. The next son became a mechanical engineer. The youngest son became a medical researcher.

Kenneth was a rural mail carrier for 33 years. When he retired, he became a full-time farmer. He raised grain and hogs. He died in 1994. He was sitting at his desk in the house he built, writing a check to their church, the First Baptist Church of Greenville, when he had a fatal stroke.

Jocelyn carried on. She stayed in the house, which remained largely the same. There were some changes, of course. The coal-burning furnace was replaced. Central air conditioning was installed.

Jocelyn got a washing machine, although she never came around to believe in dryers. The sun and the wind were good enough for her. She got a dishwasher, but she didn't use it. She spent a lot of her time gardening and fishing. She had a favorite spot, a nearby farm pond. Sometimes she fished from the bank, sometimes she used a small johnboat.

One day last fall, she was in the garden and headed up the small incline to the house. She fell. She couldn't get up. The woman who still climbed the stairs to a second-floor bedroom had run out of energy. She moved to a nursing home. She died in April.

The house and all its goods will be auctioned off Friday. I visited it this past week with the two oldest sons, Ken and Stanley. They showed me the small bedroom they shared with their two brothers. They laughed about taking baths every Wednesday and Saturday. The house seemed remarkably sturdy.

We also visited the pond where their mother used to fish. The two brothers still call it Ulmert Pond, after the family that once owned it, just as some people, I suspect, will always call the house on Eastern Avenue the Smith house.

NEXT ELECTION, LET'S ALL ELECT TO KEEP COOL OVER E-MAIL

11.12.2008

Bruce Marren will never forget the presidential election of 2008. He'd like to, but he can't. He was forced to resign this summer from his job as director of Media Resources at the Shriners Hospital for Children after sending a political e-mail from his office computer. He's still looking for work.

"I've used up all my savings. I don't think I'll make it to December," he told me this week.

His problems began in late July when a friend sent him a glowing e-mail about Barack Obama. Marren responded by sending his friend – and the other people on his friend's mailing list – an e-mail critical of Obama.

As these things go, the e-mail Marren sent was one of the more famous, or infamous, e-mails of the political season. "This is something you should be aware of so you don't get blindsided. This is going to catch a lot of families off guard," it began.

It then purportedly detailed Obama's tax plan. The e-mail said he was going to tax retirement accounts, water and electricity, end the exemption for the sale of a family home and almost double the income taxes on people making $30,000 a year. On and on it went. It would have been easy to dismiss as partisan disinformation except that it allegedly came from Robert D. Jenkins, Vice President-Investment, Chartered Retirement Planning Counselor, Wachovia Securities. His phone number and e-mail address were listed at the bottom of the e-mail.

That e-mail flashed around the Internet and was soon challenged. Almost totally false, said the various fact-checkers. Wachovia issued a statement saying that the firm did not endorse or approve the e-mail. "Members of executive and departmental leadership in Wachovia Corporation and Wachovia Securities have been made aware of the e-mail, and Robert Jenkins has been dealt with appropriately and directly. ... We sincerely apologize for this unfortunate incident."

But Marren knew only that he had received the e-mail from an attorney and that it allegedly came from an executive at Wachovia. So he passed it on to all the people who had received the glowing e-mail about Obama. One of the people on his friend's mailing list recognized that this new e-mail came from a Shriners Hospital e-mail address.

I know emotions run high during an election, but really, the Internet has become a huge garbage dump. Why get angry?

But somebody did, and that person complained to Shriners headquarters in Florida. Why is a nonprofit group sending out this kind of partisan material? Florida called St. Louis. Marren was called into Human Resources. "Don't let this happen again." No problem, he thought. He went back to work but was then told he'd have to go home while the technical people checked his computer.

"I was shocked," he said. "A little scared. I had some cartoons, some jokes. Risqué maybe, but nothing pornographic or anything. We're not supposed to use our computers for personal business, but still, I didn't think it was enough to get me fired."

Especially since he'd been there for 16 years. He had even become a Shriner.

Two days later, he was called back to work. Hospital administrator John O'Shaughnessy gave him a choice. He could resign or be fired. If he chose to resign, he'd get two weeks' severance pay. He chose to resign.

I talked to him not long after his resignation. He was in a state of shock.

"This was my whole life," he said.

He's 54. He lives on the Hill in the house in which his mother was raised. He is divorced. He has two grown children from his marriage. He has joint custody of a younger child.

I visited him recently to see if he'd found work.

"Nothing. I wake up every morning in a panic. I don't know what to do. You can't even go out looking for work anymore. It's all done online," he said.

I went to the hospital to talk with O'Shaughnessy. He said there is a policy about not using the computers for personal business, but that one e-mail would not have been enough to terminate an employee. These are difficult decisions, he said, and you have to look at a number of factors, including what is appropriate at a children's hospital. He said he hoped that Marren would get on with his life.

I called Jenkins at Wachovia.

"Sir, I am not able to speak to that subject. Would you like to talk to someone who can?"

That someone turned out to be Tony Mattera, who identified himself as a spokesman for Wachovia. He said that Jenkins had not written the e-mail but had simply passed it on. How did it have his name on it then? "Once he sent it, it went out with his auto signature. Unfortunately, that gave currency to it," Mattera said. "Obviously, he was disciplined. As we said in the statement – dealt with appropriately."

That obviously did not involve firing him, and good for Wachovia on that score. If we were to fire everybody who writes or passes along junk e-mails, nobody would be working.

Marren said he has applied for about 120 jobs. The only work he has been able to get was an Election Day gig for the Democratic Party. He passed out fliers near a polling place.

By the way, did he vote for Obama? No, he said. Ralph Nader.

THE STORY OF HOW MY CAR WENT THE WAY OF TV TUBES

5.7.2008

Perhaps I was too flippant when I wrote last week about the woman whose truck was towed into Telle Tire and Auto Service after it broke down on Interstate 44. I wrote that she arrived in town in an ignominious fashion after her old truck gave up the ghost. Hahaha. That was in the paper Friday morning.

Friday afternoon, my car did not make it off the parking lot. It started fine, made it almost to the street and then quit. The battery was fine. I kept trying to start it. Rmm, rmm, rmm. It wouldn't turn over. Rmm, rmm, rmm. I called AAA. A tow truck arrived. "It's not my battery," I said. Rmm, rmm, rmm. "Don't do that," he said. "It's probably your timing belt and if you keep trying to start the engine, you could damage it."

"I know that," I said. "I just wanted to show you." He asked where I wanted it towed. Telle Tire and Auto Service, I said. I liked the way they dealt with the woman and her truck.

Telle is not open Saturday or Sunday, so I stopped by Monday morning. A young man named John was at the service counter. His name was on his shirt, just over his pocket. I am always a little intimidated by a man whose name is on his shirt. A name on a shirt is a sign that this is a man who understands machinery. Most often, he is a repairman or a mechanic. He is competent. He is a homo sapien, and at home in the 21st century. I am not. I understand nothing about how things work. My great fear is I will be put in a time machine, taken back to an earlier time and then tortured. "We know you come from a time when there are lights. Tell us about electricity. How does it work?" "I have no idea. Arrgh!" "Tell us about cars! How do these things work?" "I have no idea. Ow!"

I tried to put my best foot forward. "I think it might be the timing belt, John."

John nodded. "It is."

That sounded good. A belt. How expensive could it be to replace a belt? Then I remembered what the tow truck driver said about trying to start the engine. "I hope there's no damage," I said defensively.

John said he didn't yet know. He said something about pistons and compression. I nodded, but the truth is, I am not entirely sure cars still have pistons. Maybe pistons went the way of the tubes that used to be in televisions. My dad used to repair televisions – his name was on his shirt – and he'd take the tubes to the grocery store where there was a tube-testing machine. When I remarked to a friend recently how odd it is that grocery stores no longer have such machines, he told me that televisions no longer have tubes. Maybe cars no longer have pistons. Maybe this is one of those inside jokes that homo sapiens use to trap Neanderthals.

"Yes, a piston. I hadn't thought of that," I said as I forced a grin.

"We can check it out if you'd like," John said. I told him to go ahead. He called a couple of hours later. He said something – the cam shaft? – had "seized up" and something else – the cam gear key way? – had been sheared. He used the kind of sympathetic tone that suggested this was very bad news.

I asked how bad it was. Very bad, he said. My only recourse would be a new engine. Well, not a new engine, but a used one. But that would be expensive, and I had to realize that my car was 12 years old and had 179,000 miles on it. I said I'd have to talk with my wife.

When a man gets to be a certain age, he starts paying close attention to the way his wife handles certain situations. How much sympathy does she have for things that are breaking down? An old car, for instance. Of course, it's not the car it once was, but we've got a lot of memories tied up in that car, and if we're willing to fork over some money, it can be put back into running condition. I explained the situation to my wife.

"Dump it," she said.

What?

"It's not worth fixing," she said.

Admittedly, I'm the sentimental one in our family, the one who cried when we took our daughter to college, the one who cried at the conclusion of our son's last high school soccer game. And yes, my wife is realistic and strong and might as well have her name on her blouse because she knows how things work, but still, it was more than a little unnerving to see how quickly she was putting the car in her rear view mirror, so to speak.

I'll think about it, I said, but what I was really doing was thinking about all the cars I've ever had and how much I miss them. Even the ones that wouldn't run. Rmm, rmm, rmm.

KINDNESSES LIFT ONE UP IN A SERIES OF DOWNS

4.17.2009

C.J. Niehoff has always been a fighter, but even the toughest scrapper can be pummeled for only so long before the legs give out.

She was sitting up in bed when I visited her at St. Anthony's Medical Center Wednesday afternoon. She was in a regular part of the hospital, not a psychiatric unit. I asked what the medical problem was. She reached down and pulled the legs of her pajamas up to show me her feet and ankles. They were badly swollen. "It's called peripheral neuropathy," she said.

That sounded sinister, but yet promising. Perhaps it could lead to some kind of disability check. I asked if she had applied for disability. She shrugged. "It's difficult to get," she said.

Niehoff was evicted from her apartment last month. She called at the time to tell me that the company that handled the eviction had stolen some of her stuff. She called later to say she was at the Hyland Behavioral Health Center at St. Anthony's. Then she called a couple of days ago to say she was in the hospital itself.

She used to work for the St. Louis Globe-Democrat. She started right out of high school in 1969. She worked in the mailroom. She used to go to O'Connell's on Thursday nights when the newspaper's Literary Club gathered. To be in the club, you had to have read a book. Any book. She aspired to be a writer.

She left the Globe in 1983 after the Herald Co. announced it was closing the paper.

I knew her only slightly. After all, I was at the other paper. So what happened? I asked her Wednesday.

She said she had a series of jobs after the Globe closed. The job she seemed most proud of was at the Racquet Club. Another St. Louis institution. The Racquet Club is where the Spirit of St. Louis was born. That's where the businessmen met and agreed to fund Lindbergh's cross-Atlantic flight.

She said she worked for the club for 14 years. Among other things, she wrote the newsletter. She said she was let go for financial reasons a few years ago. She said she was able to get only temporary work the last couple of years. In her most recent job, she was the temporary replacement for a young woman who was on maternity leave. It was the woman's first child, so Niehoff found herself hoping that the woman would decide to stay home with the baby, but that did not happen.

Without an income, she began selling her stuff on eBay, she said.

What about relatives?

None that could help, she said.

I asked where she had been living since her eviction. She said she had been sleeping in her car, a 1991 Escort. She said she had parked on the St. Anthony's parking lot. It's a safe place, she said.

She said she drove her car back and forth to the library, where she used the computers to send e-mails. The people at the library were nice.

"It's strange, but one thing about being in this position, I've been knocked sideways by how kind people have been. I mean, I've seen some rude people, but mostly people have been kind," she said.

You can start with the management at the apartment complex. "I was three months behind. They could have thrown me out long ago," she said. Her neighbors came through, too. When the eviction company put her stuff on the sidewalk, neighbors started offering her money for her stuff. She appreciated that. What else was she going to do with it? She said she made about $200. She said people at the YMCA have let her use their facilities. She knows a man who works at an Italian restaurant, and she stopped by to see him. The next thing you know she was sitting in front of a big plate of pasta.

Still, it was tough. How do these things happen? For the most part, her contemporaries are worried about their 401(k) accounts. They're living in houses. Their kids are grown. Niehoff never married. She has no family to lean on, no apartment, no stuff. She said she walked into the emergency room and announced that she was thinking about suicide. That got her into the Hyland Center.

She was released from there and her car broke down. Misfortune often comes with its own momentum. Her feet and ankles became swollen and she returned to the emergency room. She has no health insurance, but that is the least of her worries. She expects to be released any day.

As I started to leave, she gave me a piece of paper. "I wrote you a lede," she said. "The toughest part of a story is the beginning, right?"

I looked at it. It said, "C.J. Niehoff has always been a fighter, but even the toughest scrapper can only be pummeled for so long before the legs give out."

BUSINESS LEADERSHIP STYLE STEALS SUCCESS FROM ST. LOUIS

9.19.2008

A recent story in the Wall Street Journal suggested that this week's sale of Merrill Lynch to Bank of America means that the financial center of the country is shifting from New York to Charlotte, N.C.

Once again, St. Louis is left to muse, "What might have been."

You wonder what separates us from more successful cities? At its core, it is a difference in leadership. In a world of consolidation, our business leaders tend to be sellers and not buyers.

In this instance, I'm thinking of Andy Craig. He was the CEO of Boatmen's Bank. In 1996, he engineered the sale of Boatmen's to NationsBank, which a few years earlier had been North Carolina National Bank, and was to become, a few years later, Bank of America, the institution that just bought Merrill Lynch.

When Craig engineered the sale, he was 64. Ready to retire. He already had a home in Florida. What he negotiated for himself was this: $10 million in stock, a consulting job that would pay no less than $3 million a year in salary and bonuses, and then when he finally retired, $1.5 million a year for life.

What a nice retirement. In addition, if Craig were to die before his wife, she would get $1 million a year for life.

Bear in mind that Craig did not found the bank. It was nearly 140 years old when he arrived. In theory, he was just an employee, albeit the top employee.

I think it's a terrible abuse of power that somebody who doesn't own something can sell it and get himself such a sweet deal while so doing.

But hey, that's the way business works. The guys who are buying are happy to be generous to the guys who are selling because they understand that they might be on the other side of the table sometime in the future.

At any rate, in Craig, St. Louis had a guy who was ready to retire and wanted to do so in style. Charlotte had Hugh McColl, who was only a couple of years younger than Craig but was cut from a different cloth. He was a risk-taker.

So our bank ceased to exist and the bank from Charlotte continued to grow. When McColl retired, he handpicked his successor, Ken Lewis. It was Lewis who engineered the purchase of Merrill Lynch.

Of course, we've had a few risk-takers. I think of Ed Whitacre.

He ran Southwestern Bell. Then he left town and took the company with him to San Antonio. The story I heard – and repeated in print – was that he was miffed because he was unable to wrangle an invitation to join the St. Louis Country Club. In San Antonio, where he promptly joined a country club, he was a buyer and not a seller. He eventually bought AT&T.

Had Whitacre stayed here, St. Louis would have been the headquarters for AT&T.

In the spirit of full disclosure, I must confess that Susan Stiritz, the wife of William Stiritz – he was the CEO of Ralston who engineered its sale to Nestle – once came into the newspaper to complain about me. In the course of an impassioned speech, she accused me, among other things, of driving Whitacre out of town with my hateful columns.

Why is it that people who don't like me always give me too much credit? When disbarred lawyer Amiel Cueto recently filed a lawsuit accusing me, among other things, of intimidating judges, a friend from the courthouse called and said: "You could rightfully be accused of irritating judges, but not intimidating them."

In that same vein, I may have irritated Whitacre, but I didn't drive him out of town.

Fellows like him don't care about fellows like me. They care about other People of Quality. And for one reason or another, the People of Quality in this town didn't take to Whitacre.

Perhaps that's not surprising. He was a buyer, not a seller. Still, he would have brought us AT&T. It's something to think about.

Just the way this latest news about Merrill Lynch has got me thinking. What if we'd have had McColl, and Charlotte would have had Craig? Then Boatmen's would have been the bank on the move, and Nationsbank would have been looking for a buyer. Then maybe we'd have Merrill Lynch, and the Wall Street Journal would be saying that the financial center of the country is shifting to St. Louis.

It's all about leadership.

By the way, several months before Craig engineered the sale of Boatmen's Bank, he was named St. Louis Man of the Year.

FAMILY ANCHOR HAS DISPENSED DISCIPLINE, FAITH AND LOVE

9.24.2006

Viola Austin was born in Kansas almost 70 years ago. She was the middle child of five. Her father was a coal miner. Her mother earned extra money cooking for other families. Viola's parents divorced, and her mother remarried and moved the family to St. Louis when Viola was 9.

The family was working-class, but barely. Viola stayed in high school through the 11th grade and then dropped out to go to work. She got a job sterilizing equipment at the Washington University medical school. She got married and had six children. She got divorced.

She became a seamstress. She worked for the Great Western Bag Company, and when that company moved to Tennessee, she found other work. When she was lucky, she could do her sewing at home and watch the kids. By the way, all of her kids stayed out of trouble. They grew up, got married, got jobs. For the most part, they climbed into the middle class.

Things went haywire in 1986. One of Viola's daughters, Marvina Mayweather, who worked at a cocktail lounge on Vandeventer, got into a relationship with an older man. She was 26. He was 51. Marvina tried to break up with him, but she was afraid. Viola met him and talked with him. Don't hurt my daughter, she said. But he did. He shot her in the head. He then shot himself, but he flinched as he pulled the trigger, and he did not die. He was later convicted of first-degree murder. He is now 70 and still in prison. The newspaper account of the crime said that Marvina was trying to get a court order to keep him away.

Marvina left two young daughters, and Viola took them in. One of her sisters had died shortly before Marvina was murdered, and Viola had taken in her youngest child. He was a teenager.

As she had done with her own kids, Viola kept everybody on the straight and narrow.

Marvina's oldest daughter, Toya Like, was 8 when she moved in with her grandmother. She was good at school. She was on the drill team at Beaumont High School. Viola sewed the uniforms. Toya earned a scholarship to the University of Missouri at St. Louis. She graduated with a degree in criminology in 1999.

I wrote a column about her. I wrote that she took the bus down Vandeventer right past the cocktail lounge where her mother used to work. Then, as often happens, I lost touch with her.

About a week ago, I got a call from Viola. Toya just earned her doctorate, she said.

Viola used to live in a two-family flat on the North Side, but she has now moved into a low-income apartment building on the Near South Side. It's a nice place, and, of course, Viola's apartment is well-kept. She told me she was in the back of the room when Toya defended her dissertation in August.

Toya is the first of the family to get through college, and there were times when that seemed unlikely. While she was an undergraduate, she had a baby. That could have been the end of college for Toya, but she was determined, and so was Viola. One required class was offered only at night, and Toya would rush from school to the day-care center and then back to campus with the baby. Viola would get off work and rush to campus and take her great-granddaughter from her granddaughter just as the class began.

While Toya is the academic star of the family, everybody else is doing fine, too. I asked Viola how she did it.

"I was kind of strict," she said. "I didn't believe in them running the streets."

Plus, there was a heavy dose of faith. Viola is a longtime member of St. John Church of God in Christ.

"I really believe in the Lord," she said.

Toya is working in Kansas City. I called her office and got her answering machine.

"You've reached Doctor Toya Like at the Department of Sociology, Criminal Justice and Criminology at the University of Missouri Kansas City."

Doctor Toya Like. That has a nice sound, especially to Viola Austin.

Bill McClellan • Gently Down the Stream

DRUG WAR CASUALTY STIRS MORE REFLECTION

11.8.2008

Alejandro Murillo came to federal court Thursday morning wearing a gray-and-white striped shirt and pants outfit with Phelps County Jail stenciled on the back of the shirt. In these lean times, an enterprising county can make a nice piece of change housing federal prisoners.

Murillo was one of several people scheduled for sentencing, and I looked around at the other spectators and wondered if any of them were there for him. A few feet to the right of me sat a young woman who seemed to be fighting back tears. Perhaps she is here for Murillo, I thought. Maybe she is Zenaida Alcazar.

Murillo and Alcazar were driving east on Interstate 44 when they pulled into a truck stop near Rolla late one night in April. They got into a heated argument in the cab of their truck and Murillo chased Alcazar into the convenience store. The clerk called the police. When the cops began to question the couple, alarm bells went off. I-44 is a major thoroughfare in the drug world, and here was a couple from Arizona driving a truck and trailer with Kentucky plates.

The cops asked for permission to search the truck and trailer. No, said Murillo. The cops called for a drug dog. Ziggy the drug dog took one sniff at the trailer and began to bark.

The trailer contained 855 pounds of pot. Murillo was charged. Alcazar was released.

I wrote a lighthearted column about the folly of arguing with a woman.

Eventually, Murillo pleaded guilty to possession of marijuana with intent to distribute.

He's 32 years old. He has four kids. He was going to make $10,000 for transporting the dope. That's tax-free money, of course. No Social Security taxes, no Medicare taxes, no income taxes. The government gets nothing.

Murillo stood at the lectern facing the judge. To his left was his federal defender, and to the left of his federal defender was the assistant U.S. attorney.

I have known both of them for a long time. They are good and decent men. For that matter, I like the judge, too. The lawyers, the judge and I are all baby boomers.

I looked at the scene in front of me, and I thought, "What happened?"

There was a time, long ago, when I thought my generation was going to change things. Maybe we'd never be called the Greatest Generation, but at least we'd bring a more sensible approach to drug laws. At the very least, we'd legalize pot.

In fact, I remember people talking about how the tobacco companies were buying land in Mexico, and how they had already copyrighted pot names. "R.J. Reynolds already has Acapulco Gold," is the sort of thing people would say. That made sense. Those were the days when you couldn't walk into a party without somebody handing you a joint.

When we got the power, we'd change things.

You know how that worked out. The first boomer president said he didn't inhale, and the second boomer president pulled a Mark McGwire and said he wasn't here to talk about the past. And that was that. Two and out. It was as if somebody said, "Don't Bogart the torch." We passed it to the next generation.

I find much about the drug laws hard to believe. When I was a kid, the mob ran the numbers game. Then the government saw it for the cash cow it was, took it away from the mob and called it the lottery. Why don't we want the revenue from marijuana?

The judge asked Murillo if he had anything to say before sentencing. Murillo said he wanted to turn his life around. "This is the lowest point. I don't want go lower than this," he said.

Murillo is a good case study in two respects. First, drugs are bad. Drugs have messed up his life. He got a bad conduct discharge from the Navy because of drugs. Then he got hooked on crystal meth. So yes, his experiences tell us that drugs, like booze and like gambling, can ruin a person. But he messed up his life while drugs were illegal, and that tells us the second thing – prohibition doesn't work.

It's like we have a choice. We can have Gussie Busch, or we can have Al Capone.

By the way, Murillo was offered a deal by the feds. He could get a lighter sentence if he told them who hired him to deliver the dope. He did not take the deal. We can only guess at his reasoning.

The day before Murillo was sentenced, retired Brig. Gen. Juan Arturo Esparza was assassinated. He was the police chief of a town in northern Mexico. He had taken office four days earlier.

The judge gave Murillo 37 months. That was at the low end of the sentencing guidelines.

As I left the courtroom, I glanced at the young woman who had been sitting to my right. She was still there, still waiting. Her tears were not for Murillo.

FARM GIRL FEARED COWS BUT BECAME EARLY RISER

3.3.2010

Among the worshippers at the weekday 6:30 a.m. Mass at All Souls Catholic Church in Overland is a friend of mine. "I do this not because I am holy, but simply because I am a reprobate always in recovery," he said.

He does not make it every day. A woman who sits in the back pew has noticed his imperfect attendance and sometimes asks if he has been ill. She occasionally misses a day herself, so my friend turned the table on her the other morning and asked if she had been sick. "No," she said. "Sometimes the papers are late."

She is a newspaper carrier.

Her name is Anne Elmore. She is 73. She was raised on a dairy farm in De Soto. It was a large farm, 500 acres or so, and it came to her family through a land grant shortly after the Civil War. Anne grew up doing all the chores one might expect a farm child to do - except for milking the cows. "I was afraid of them," she said.

She wanted to be a doctor. She went to the University of Missouri in Columbia and took pre-med courses. While she was away at college, her father was killed in an accident. He fell off a horse-drawn wagon, which then ran over him. This was in 1956 so he did not have to use horses in the field, but he was old-fashioned and preferred them.

Anne graduated the next year. She married a young man she had met at the university. He became a salesman. Anne forgot about medical school and started having children. She had nine of them.

Shortly after the last of their children was born, Anne and her husband separated. Later, they divorced, and Anne received an annulment from the church.

She decided to get a degree in medical technology. With her credits from Missouri, she figured it would not take her long. It did not. She went to Fontbonne and got a degree. Her husband paid child support and Anne's mother and aunt, both of whom are now deceased, helped with the children.

Anne worked for about 10 years at Missouri Baptist Hospital. She liked the work - she was a chemistry supervisor - but she was trying to raise a house full of children and she felt like she needed a job that would let her be home when the kids got out of school.

She knew some people in her Maryland Heights neighborhood who were newspaper carriers. They were home all day. That sounded like the job for her.

In those days - 25 years ago - newspaper routes were independent businesses. People owned them. Anne heard of a route that was for sale. It covered parts of St. Ann, Overland and Breckenridge Hills. The price for the route was $70,000.

Anne borrowed the money. She delivered about 750 papers Monday through Saturday and a little more than 1,000 on Sunday.

It was late night, early morning work, and it meant that Anne was home for her children.

Also, it was lucrative. In her best years, she made about $60,000, she said. All of the kids went to Catholic schools.

The business has changed. The newspaper now owns routes. Anne sold her route to the newspaper about five years ago but continued to work it.

She now makes about $40,000 a year, she said. She gets no benefits.

She gets up each morning about 1:15. She leaves her house about 1:50 and drives to a distribution site in North County to pick up her papers. She puts her papers together and rolls them and is on her route shortly before 3. She is supposed to be done by 5:30, and she usually is.

She delivers about 550 Post-Dispatch newspapers daily and about 700 on Sunday. The route also includes the Wall Street Journal - she has about 10 subscribers on her route - and the Suburban Journals. She delivers about 150 of them. She drives a 2001 Chevy van.

It is, of course, a seven-day-a-week job. I asked what happens if she is sick. "I've never been sick," she said. One of her sons used to help with the route and cover for her if she wanted to take a day off. She said her last day off was about five years ago.

When the newspapers aren't late, she makes the 6:30 Mass in Overland. If the newspapers are late, she makes the 8 a.m. Mass at Holy Spirit near her house in Maryland Heights.

Then she comes home, has breakfast and naps for a couple of hours. On Mondays, she goes to DePaul Health Center, where she visits Catholic patients and brings them Holy Communion.

She is usually in bed before 9 p.m. in preparation for the day that begins at 1:15 a.m.

That's an hour when even cows are asleep.

CUETO SUIT PAINTS ME AS A GUY WITH POWER

9.14.2008

I was walking toward the newspaper building Thursday morning when a man jumped out of a parked car and approached me. He had a gun holstered at his side. "You're Bill McClellan, aren't you?"

I saw no point in denying the truth. "Yes," I said. He handed me some papers. Oh, good. A process server. So much better than an angry reader.

Another lawsuit.

I glanced at it as I walked into the building. It was an excellent lawsuit. Not just the usual libel and slander. This one included "intimidation of judges and witnesses." I am not certain I have been accused of that before. Clearly, this was the product of a fertile legal mind.

That mind belongs to Amiel Cueto.

Regular readers are familiar with him. He was once a very big deal in St. Clair and Madison counties' legal community. Also, in the Democratic Party on the east side. He is a longtime chum of Congressman Jerry Costello. He was the best man at Costello's wedding, and Costello was best man at his.

The last time I saw Cueto was in August of last year. He was suing The Record, a newspaper that covers legal affairs in Madison and St. Clair counties. The newspaper had run a gossipy item alleging that Cueto had been seen at a meeting of St. Clair County judges at a restaurant in Belleville. The item said that during his heyday, he was "said to have owned" many judges.

I attended a hearing in connection with his lawsuit against The Record. I wrote about it. I was very careful. That's because Cueto is a disbarred lawyer. He can represent only himself. So if he wants to practice law, he has to sue people. Aware of this, I hedged everything, even my description of him as he sat in the courtroom. "His stomach was allegedly lopping over his pants. His hair was long, but allegedly thin on top. His mustache was allegedly wispy." Yes, I was on my best behavior.

But it wasn't enough. Cueto did not enjoy the column. He sent a letter to one of the lawyers representing The Record. Cueto wrote that he intended to call me as a witness at the trial. He wrote that I was an agent of The Record, and acting in that capacity, I had written a column filled with lies in an effort to thwart Cueto's lawsuit. He also mentioned that he intended to pursue other litigation at a later time.

Oh, no, I thought. He might mean me.

Turns out he did.

I read his lawsuit with great interest. It took a while. He does not save his arguments for the courtroom. He puts them right into the lawsuit. For instance, he went into some detail about me.

"McClellan is a self-admitted thief. See Exhibit 3, which is a column published on March 14, 2008, in which McClellan bragged about conspiracy with others to steal money out of women's purses. McClellan has also written columns in which he has bragged about conspiracy with his father in the bribery of police officers."

Actually, he referred to many of my columns. In a strange way, I was touched. We need all the readers we can get.

He even mentioned some nice things I have written about him. He said I once wrote that he was "almost heroic." And yes, by gosh, I did. I was describing the scene in which the assistant U.S. attorney was approaching him to begin her cross-examination during his trial. He was charged with obstruction of justice and conspiracy to obstruct justice. I wrote that I had always thought of Cueto as a bully, but suddenly he seemed transformed. "Suddenly, he seemed almost heroic. Slouched in his chair, he was cloaked in the same sort of nobility that comes naturally to a treed animal. How can you root against such a creature as it stares down impassively at the hounds baying beneath it?"

Of course, all of our history is fine and good, but what about these new allegations. How had I intimidated judges and witnesses?

That goes back to The Record's story that started this whole thing. The Record reported that Cueto had been seen at a meeting of the judges on Jan. 19, 2006. Eight of the judges, including Cueto's brother Lloyd, signed a letter to the paper saying the story wasn't true. In fact, they didn't even have a meeting on Jan. 19. It turns out the meeting was on Jan. 18 and, according to an affidavit from one of the judges who had signed the letter, Cueto did stop by the meeting. So what was the truth?

I wrote, "How can any judge in St. Clair County possibly handle a case in which the veracity of one or more of his colleagues is at issue?"

That was the intimidation!

Cueto's lawsuit says my column caused the case to be assigned to somebody outside St. Clair County. Also, I used my power to "deter Circuit Judges of St. Clair County from testifying freely, fully and truthfully." I have that sort of power over the judges?

I'd hate to lose a lawsuit, but geez, I like the sound of Cueto's argument.

WATCHING DREAMS UNRAVEL

1.25.2009

In the summer of 2003, Noe Guzman and his family – his mom, stepfather and baby sister – moved to New Haven from a small town in Michigan. Noe (pronounced Noah) had just turned 12 and was entering seventh grade. That might be a rough age to enter a new school – especially a small school where everybody has known everybody forever – but it didn't seem to bother Noe. He was the only Hispanic kid in the class, but that didn't bother him, either. He quickly made friends, and when he graduated two years later, he was salutatorian of the class.

High school has been more of the same. Now in the second semester of his senior year, he has been on the honor roll every semester. "He has an outstanding record of academics here," said Rhonda Helling, a teacher at New Haven High School.

He has also been a pretty good cross-country runner. This year, though, he needed gallbladder surgery and couldn't run. That didn't stop him from supporting the team. "A lot of kids, if they couldn't compete, would just drop out," said John Tucker, the cross country coach and a history teacher. "But not Noe. He became the manager. He made sure the runners had water, and he was our biggest cheerleader."

Noe also is a member of the student council and of the Future Business Leaders of America.

He wants to be a doctor. In other words, Noe is a small-town kid with big dreams. Sadly, Noe's dreams are in the process of unraveling. That process began when Noe decided to join the Marine Corps.

By the way, the Marine Corps is filled with young men from small towns who decided that the service was a way to kick-start their dreams. That's why the Marines send recruiters to small-town high schools. When the recruiters visited New Haven High, they set up a pull-up bar. Do 20 pull-ups and get a Marine

Corps T-shirt. Noe did 22 pull-ups. "Have you ever thought about the Marine Corps?" a recruiter asked.

Yes, he had. "I love adventure," he told me last week.

So this summer he went to the recruiter in nearby Washington and said he'd like to sign up for a delayed enlistment. He'd head to boot camp once he graduated from high school in May. No problem. The recruiter drove him to St. Louis to take the Armed Services Vocational Aptitude Battery test. Noe did very well.

He returned Aug. 13 to take his physical. He was at the Robert Young Federal Building with other young people in the process of enlisting when a man in civilian clothes led Noe to a room. "Did you really think you could get away with this?" he asked.

"He looked angry," Noe said. "I almost laughed. I think I said, 'You must have the wrong guy.'"

Noe said the man told him to stand up and put his hands behind his back. The man handcuffed him, then shackled his feet. "Do you know what kind of trouble you're in?" he asked Noe. He led Noe to another room.

A man from Immigration and Customs Enforcement was in the second room. Noe said he was calm and polite. The military had collected all of Noe's identification, and now the man from ICE put Noe's Social Security card in front of him. "This number does not belong to you," he said.

Noe didn't understand. He had used that Social Security number for work purposes. He had used that number when he filed taxes.

The man from ICE told Noe he was an illegal alien. Noe was stunned. He knew he had been born in Mexico; he had a vague memory of moving to the States with his mother at age 4. But illegally? The man from ICE told Noe that he could deport him right then. But he didn't. Instead, he told Noe to call his mother.

She drove to St. Louis. She told Noe that yes, he was an illegal immigrant. Your father was abusive, and I needed to get us away from him, she said. She had purchased the Social Security card once they arrived in this country.

Noe was released on his own recognizance. He was given a court date in October, and then one in December. Both times, he appeared without a lawyer – his mother and stepfather have little money. He now has a court date in February.

I visited him Wednesday after school. I asked if he were really completely surprised when he learned he was here illegally. "Oh yes," he said. "I never had any doubt I was a citizen."

He said he had been told he had little chance of avoiding deportation. He said he had been told he would need to meet three criteria – 10 years' residence in this country, no criminal record and somebody dependent upon him. He said nobody was dependent upon him.

He has an appointment Monday with a lawyer named Katie Herbert Meyer. She works for Interfaith Legal Service. I called her Friday afternoon. I told her what Noe had said about the criteria he would need to meet to stay in this country. Maybe if he had gotten married instead of trying to enlist he'd be all right, I said.

No, she said, a person facing deportation can file an application for cancellation of removal. That requires 10 years of residence, good moral character, a qualifying family member – parent, spouse or child – who is a citizen or a lawful permanent resident. Finally, the applicant must demonstrate that there would be an "exceptional and extremely unusual" hardship to that family member if the applicant were to be deported. Meyer said immigration judges were very strict when interpreting hardships.

It does not sound like Noe would qualify, I said.

Meyer said she had not been hired but would explore the situation when they met Monday for the initial consultation. "He is the exact type of person who would be helped if the Congress would pass the DREAM Act," she said.

The Developmment, Relief and Education for Alien Minors Act was introduced in 2005 and would provide a path to legal residency for young people brought here as children, who fulfill requirements such as graduating from high school and attending college or serving in the military.

There is little chance of that passing in two weeks, I said.

"This is part of the broken immigration system you hear about," she said.

I spoke with Carl Rusnok, the director of communciations for the central region of ICE. He said he could only confirm that Noe Guzman was referred to ICE after a Military Entrance Processing Station determined his Social Security number was fraudulent, and that his immigration hearing was scheduled for Feb. 3.

Noe said the waiting was tough. "Every day I look at the calendar and I think it might be another day closer to the last day I can be with my friends."

TOWN RALLIES FOR IMMIGRANT TEEN CHASING DREAM

3.11.2009

"Our fax machine is out of ink," said Katie Herbert Meyer, legal director of Interfaith Legal Services for Immigrants. She was referring to the outpouring of support she has received for Noe Guzman, a 17-year-old from New Haven who learned he was an illegal alien when he tried to join the Marine Corps last year.

Noe (pronounced Noah) is a small-town kid with big dreams. He wants to be a doctor. His family does not have a lot of money, so he decided to go into the military after he graduates from high school this May. He'd then use the educational benefits to go to college and medical school. He opted for the Marine Corps. He came to St. Louis in August to complete his enlistment. But something was wrong with his Social Security card, the one he had used for part-time jobs after school. It turned out to be bogus. What's more, he was an illegal alien. He was suddenly facing deportation.

Talk about falling into a rabbit hole. Noe barely remembered coming to this country when he was 4. He had grown up assuming that he and his mother had come here legally. "I thought for sure I was a citizen. I didn't even think about it," he told me. He and his mom lived in a small town in Michigan. They moved to New Haven in 2003 when Noe was going into seventh grade.

He did fine in school. He ran cross-country. He participated in extracurricular activities. He had part-time jobs. He was popular. He had a girlfriend. He was a typical American kid. No, not typical. Exemplary.

He eventually got a lawyer from Interfaith Legal Services for Immigrants who gave him some bad news. There isn't a whole lot we can do, she explained.

A person facing deportation can file an application for cancellation of removal, but that requires, among other things, that the applicant demonstrate that a family member who is a citizen or a lawful permanent resident would face an exceptional hardship if the applicant were to be deported. So maybe if Noe would have dropped out of high school and fathered a couple of kids, he'd have been all right. But he took another path – he stayed in school and then decided to join the Marines.

When news of Noe's plight got out, the people of New Haven rallied to his side. They asked Meyer, What can we do? Letters might help, she said. About all we can do is ask the chief counsel of Immigration and Customs Enforcement to exercise prosecutorial discretion and terminate the removal proceedings, she said.

New Haven is not San Francisco. It's small-town America. In the truest sense of the word, it's a conservative place. It's represented in the state Legislature by Rep. Charlie Schlottach. According to the official manual of the state, he's the owner-operator of a 200 cow-calf operation on a fifth-generation family farm. He's a Republican and a member of the Owensville Gun Club, the American Wild Turkey Federation and the Gasconade County Bible Society. Those are not the credentials of a bleeding-heart liberal.

But Schlottach has been strong in support of Noe. Here is an excerpt from Schlottach's letter. "We have a young man who wants to fight to become an American; a young man who has met and surpassed the American standard of work, willing to obey this country's laws. A young man who has the support of every teacher, school administrator, fellow student and community member I have encountered. ... I offer my whole-hearted support to Noe and his quest to gain American citizenship."

My favorite letter came from a woman who described herself as a lifelong resident of New Haven: "I never expected to write a letter concerning immigrant rights. In my mind, the situation was quite clear; a person was either a U.S. citizen or he wasn't. That seems simple enough. However, Noe Guzman's situation brings up a facet of immigrant rights that I hadn't previously considered – those of immigrant children. Young immigrant children don't have a choice in whether or not they enter this country. Once here, they grow up learning to love the United States just like other children. They enroll in our schools and become a part of us.

"You may look at Noe Guzman and see an illegal immigrant. That's not what I see. I see Noe, the boy who sang a solo as the Cowardly Lion in a middle school musical; Noe, the boy who was the salutatorian of his 8th grade class; Noe, the lifeguard at the city pool; and most recently, Noe, the kind young man I ran into at the veterinarian's office who offered to carry my dying Labrador retriever to my car.

"I can no longer look at immigration in shades of black and white or in terms of right and wrong."

All told, about 40 people sent letters, and about 300 people signed a petition.

Noe's hearing was Tuesday. He was accompanied by his mother, who is also facing deportation, and his girlfriend's mother, Sandy Bockting, whose daughter, Alexis, also wants to be a doctor. The hearing lasted only moments. Noe won. That is, the chief counsel of ICE agreed to terminate the removal proceedings. Noe will graduate with his class in May. But what then? He will have no legal status. He can't go to a public college in Missouri, and he can't join the military.

Meyer said the only hope is something called a private bill. Somebody from Congress would have to sponsor a bill that would grant him permanent lawful residence. Then he could join the military and start on a path toward the citizenship he once assumed he had.

TRUE STORY: WOMAN WAS MOBSTER'S DAUGHTER

6.1.2007

It is so a small world. Susan Jansen is the daughter of Lou Shoulders. Her body was found eight days ago at a St. Louis recycling center. Her injuries were consistent with having been smashed by the compactor of a recycling truck, and police theorized that she may have fallen asleep in a collection bin. The story that appeared in this paper said her maiden name was Shoulders.

A reader with a memory called me. "Lou had a daughter named Susan," she said.

So I called the county police, and a detective said, "Wrong family." I then wrote a column recalling the history of the Shoulders family. "In a small world, Susan Jansen would have been Lou Shoulders' daughter," I wrote.

Friends and acquaintances of Susan's called to tell me she was Lou's daughter. It was easy to verify. Arrest records trace her back to the days when she lived with her mother, Shirley, who became a widow when Louis D. Shoulders was killed by a car bomb in August 1972.

He was a suspect in a number of mob-related murders. Police speculated that he had been killed in retaliation for the earlier murder of the business manager of Pipefitters Local 562. Shoulders had been on the union payroll as a bodyguard. His funeral was a big event among local organized crime figures. Newspaper photographers jostled with police photographers outside the funeral home.

But when it comes to notoriety, Louis D. Shoulders never escaped his father's shadow. Louis Ira Shoulders was a lieutenant in the St. Louis Police Department. He was known as "The Shadow." He was courageous and crooked. He killed two men in the line of duty. He was also involved in prostitution and gambling. He eventually went to prison for lying to a grand jury about the whereabouts of $300,000 of ransom money from the Bobby Greenlease kidnapping.

That money was never recovered. Authorities speculated that it had been shipped to mobsters in Chicago.

Perhaps it is not surprising that the lieutenant's son became a mobster. But what happened to the mobster's daughter?

First of all, the mob doesn't have a pension plan. I remember visiting Eunice Flynn a few years ago. Her husband, Raymond Flynn, had once been a big deal, and Eunice had worn diamonds and furs. But when I visited her, Raymond had been in prison for 16 years, and she was driving a bus for the Special School District.

Shirley Shoulders may not have driven a bus after her husband got blown up in his Cadillac, but friends say she lived modestly. She and Susan shared a one-bedroom condo.

"Sue was a kind woman who made bad choices in her life," one of her friends told me.

Some of those choices had to do with drugs. Her scrapes with the law seem to revolve around drugs. Her husband, Thomas Jansen, seemed to share some of those same problems.

"I've known Susan and Tom for 25 years," one man told me. He said that Jansen was a pastry chef and that Susan worked a series of low-paying jobs. "I lost touch a couple of years ago when Tom got in trouble for heroin," the man said. Records show a drug possession conviction in 2000, and then a probation revocation in '04. Jansen was sent to the County Jail in Clayton.

County police have patched together the last month or so of Susan's life. She and Jansen were evicted from their apartment early in the month but stayed with a friend in the complex. On the 23rd of last month, they were asked to leave. Police were called.

The couple walked to another friend's house, but their erratic behavior unnerved him. Susan was talking to the walls. Jansen seemed suicidal. They left their friend's house and were last seen about 2 a.m. They were on foot. Their belongings were in a duffel bag that they had put in a shopping cart. The house they left was approximately four blocks from a newspaper recycling bin on St. Johns Church road. A driver picked up the papers from the recycling bin early Thursday morning.

Susan, who was a short woman, was known to panhandle in the area near that recycling bin. I think of her panhandling, and I think of the description of her grandfather: "The elder Shoulders was a police lieutenant who was more than 6 feet, 2 inches tall," according to a previous article by this newspaper. "He was bow-legged and walked with a rolling gait. He feared no man, being handy with his fists and his revolver."

Police are awaiting toxicology tests on Susan. They still hope to locate Jansen to make sure he's all right.

Bill McClellan • Gently Down the Stream

FAMILY-OWNED BUSINESS GREASES GEARS OF HISTORY

11.16.2008

The economic downturn is playing havoc with a lot of businesses, but the folks at Schaeffer's Manufacturing don't seem concerned. After all, their company has survived perilous times before. Like the Great Fire of '49. That's '49 as in 1849.

A fire began on a steamboat, spread to 23 other steamers, jumped to the piles of freight on the levee and eventually burned down a good chunk of what is now Laclede's Landing, which is where Schaeffer's was then located. The only piece of equipment from Schaeffer's that survived the Great Fire was a hammer, and it is now on display in the lobby of the company's present location on Barton Street just south of downtown.

The fire did not stop Nicholas Schaeffer, the German immigrant who had founded the company in 1839. It was, in those days, a manufacturer of soap, candles and axle grease. For those of us who have grown up with electricity, it's hard to fathom how important candles once were. Speaking of the California gold rush, people at Schaeffer said, "We lit the way."

It was another Schaeffer's product, Black Beauty Grease, that lubricated the wheels of the wagon trains that headed west, and yet another Schaeffer's product, Red Engine Oil, that lubricated the steamboats.

Schaeffer lost much of his personal fortune in the Panic of 1870, but the company survived. When Schaeffer died in 1880, his son, Jacob, took over. He led the company into the age of electricity, which was not a godsend for candlemakers. Jacob's son-in-law, William Shields, led the company through the Great Depression.

The fourth generation, Tom and Gwynne Shields, took over after World War II. Tom had been a glider pilot during the war, and he knew that the Army Air

Forces was using a metal, molybdenum, in its lubricants. Schaeffer's followed suit and the company, which had nearly gone under in the Depression, began to grow again.

Grease was then the name of the game. Grease to lubricate the machinery that was building the postwar world. Fortunately, Schaeffer's had a genius of a grease-man, Mike Ryterski. He started at Schaeffer's in 1940. He served in the Army Air Forces during the war and returned to Schaeffer's afterward. He developed a grease for gears that operate in open air. Shell Oil tried to duplicate it, could not and eventually signed an agreement with Schaeffer's to use Ryterski's product, Silver Streak, all over the world. Ryterski is now 89 years old, and he still comes to work three days a week. He heads research and development.

He grew up on a farm in Illinois near Pinckneyville. He finished seventh grade. How could a man with a seventh-grade education come up with a product that Shell's engineers could not duplicate?

He shrugged. How did it come about? He said that a salesman was selling to coal mines and complained to him that the grease for the heavy machinery wasn't getting the job done. The gears were not enclosed. "So I started in thinking we needed a heavier oil that wouldn't squeeze out in the air," he said, as if it ought to make sense to anybody. "So I just started mixing."

He does not have a desk. He works on his feet. To illuminate his work space, he pulled a string, and a moment later, an overhead fluorescent light came on.

That might seem a little odd, a little dated. Well, if you go to the vending machine on the production floor, you can buy a Coke for 15 cents.

Yet, in 1998, the RCGA named Schaeffer's one of the 50 fastest growing high-tech companies in the area. And it was, and is, fast-growing, and the world of specialized lubricants is indeed high-tech. People in labs are checking viscosity and purity and new additives are being developed.

Still, it seemed old-fashioned when I visited last week. "This is our new plant. It was built in 1880," said company chairman, John Schaeffer Shields. He and his sister, the late Jackie Schaeffer Hermann, took over the company in 1982 when their brother, Tom, died. Gwynne died earlier.

One of the first things Shields and his sister did was put 51 percent of the family-owned stock in an irrevocable trust for the next 100 years. That would ensure, Shields explained, that the company cannot be sold. The notion of family business is taken seriously. In fact, Schaeffer's is the oldest family-owned business in Missouri.

Shields' son, Jay, is the company president. Hermann's son, Tom, is the CEO. Tom's daughter, Jill, who represents the sixth generation, is head of quality control. Her cousin, Will Gregerson, is comptroller and treasurer. The offices are very modest. None of the executives have a secretary. The atmosphere is informal. Many of the staffers I met said they have been there for years. Some have children working there.

Every month is a new record sales month. Schaeffer's lubricants are sold in 55 countries. Sales are expected to hit $100 million next year.

The phones are not automated. "Oh, I hate that 'press one, press two' thing," said Shields. If you call, you get a person. Debbie Townsend answers the phone. "And everybody takes phone calls, even if they're in meetings," she said.

There are about 55 people working in the office, and about 25 in the production facility. There are more than 500 salesmen.

"People come here, they tend to stay for years," said Shields.

Have there been many offers to buy the company?

"Dozens of requests," said Shields. "We're not interested. I always explain that we have that irrevocable trust. We're planning on keeping this going indefinitely."

STRANGERS GIVE MAN
NEW HOPE, THEN FATE STEPS IN

1.20.2008

I returned from vacation on Jan. 4 and started reading the e-mails that had accumulated in my absence. I read them chronologically. The first batch was from before Christmas. One was from Michael Halwe. He had written a note at 5:51 a.m. on Christmas Eve. He said he had just read that morning's column – it was about him – and he liked it. Except I had gotten the sex of one of his dogs wrong. I had referred to Magic as "he."

"I now have 98 pounds of upset FEmale Labrador," he wrote. On a more serious note, he had good news. "The state of Missouri has determined that I am disabled. I got the letter Saturday."

That news fell into the category of good things happening to good people. Halwe was a bowler. He had competed on the regional tour. Then he managed a couple of bowling centers – "Don't call them bowling alleys!" – and then he worked for, and eventually bought, a company that sold bowling balls, shoes, bags and so on. The company was not doing well. People were going on the Internet and buying directly from the manufacturers. Because his company was crumbling, he had no health insurance. He had serious health problems and had suffered two heart attacks early last year. He was 49 years old.

Things went from bad to worse. In late October, he was about to lose his house. He was desperate. He had no family – just two dogs. "I have no idea where my dogs and I will be going," he wrote me in an e-mail. He did not respond to e-mails, and his phone seemed to be out of service. I heard from him again in early December. "I've been saved," he said.

A fellow dog owner had saved him. One of his dogs was a bearded collie, and Michael was active in the bearded collie world. He did volunteer work for bearded collie rescue – his own bearded collie, Morgan, had come from the Humane Society – and he was a regular at the bearded collie camp held every other year at

Purina Farms in Gray Summit. He chatted regularly with other bearded collie owners on the Internet. During one of these chats, he mentioned his problems to Larry Abramson of Olive Branch, Miss. Two days later, a bearded collie owner from Kentucky contacted Halwe. "How much do you need?" she asked. "Could I borrow $2,000?" he responded. "No, I'll give you $2,000," she said. She did.

Halwe used that to stave off the foreclosure. He was optimistic about his pending application for disability. "I think I'm going to make it," he told me.

That was the Christmas Eve column. The kindness of strangers.

I was glad to see that Halwe liked the column. And his disability had been approved. That was good news. I continued going through the e-mails. I came to January 3rd. Several people sent me the same message. "Michael Halwe had a heart attack and died."

I went back and read the Christmas Eve e-mail. Also, another e-mail Halwe had sent two days earlier, shortly after I had last met with him. He said some Internet friends from a sports chat room had collected money for him, too. "All of this is almost too much to imagine," he wrote. "I'm a very introverted cynic who has always believed that the milk of human kindness was way past its expiration date. For people who don't even know me to help, it just overwhelms me."

That was a nice thought. Life was not always kind to Halwe. His wife died in an auto accident years ago. His only sibling died of cancer. His own health went bad so early. But at the end, things seemed to be breaking his way. That's something.

After Halwe's death, friends put his two dogs in a kennel. They were hoping to find somebody who would adopt them together – a 13-year-old bearded collie and a 9-year-old Lab with epilepsy.

But one week after Halwe's death, the bearded collie died. A friend of Michael's sent me an e-mail. "A front leg was swollen twice its normal size. He couldn't walk on his back legs at all. The doctor suspected bone cancer. It was time to let him go. Morgan will be cremated and will be laid to rest with his beloved Michael."

Halwe's friends had a memorial service for him on Monday. Nearly 100 people attended. Some were from his bowling life. Some knew him from the Internet. Others were from the world of bearded collies. Everybody talked about his sense of humor, and the way he persevered even when things didn't go well. A friend who helped him publish a book of poetry read some of his poems.

One of Halwe's friends approached me at the service. "If you write something, could you mention that Magic needs a home? We have a benefactor who will pay for her medication."

Sure, I said.

By the way, Magic turned 9 on Christmas Eve. Halwe wrote an e-mail about that, too. "As she's gotten older, the white mascara on her black face keeps creeping further around her eyes. She has white eyelashes! She realizes that Morgan is getting feeble and she tries to help him along. The epilepsy hasn't seemed to affect her outlook on life. She's still the happy-go-lucky Labrador that I brought home nine years ago. Happy birthday, Magic. Hope we both have nine more."

DAUGHTER ISN'T BUYING THEORY ABOUT EMPTY ROADS

2.22.2008

My daughter came home for a visit. She teaches high school biology in California. She believes in evolution. Furthermore, she is not only convinced that the world is more than 6,000 years old, she thinks it's round.

I try not to argue with her. If she wants to be a Democrat, that's up to her.

I had to take her to the airport Thursday morning. Whenever I go to the airport, I think about the round-earth theory.

Many years ago, I flew to what should have been the other side of the globe. Did the airplane ever have to fly upside down? No.

Yet, if you take a globe and then pretend your hand is a plane and move it around to the other side of the globe, your hand ends up upside down. That's not a theory, either. It's a scientific fact.

Had I home-schooled my children, they would understand this. Instead, I sent them to public schools. Still, I try to let them know there are two sides to these issues. In that sense, the drive to the airport represented a teaching moment.

"What do you think of the traffic?" I asked her.

"Not bad, Dad. You should try to get around in California."

Actually, the traffic wasn't too bad, and that was my point. We were headed north on Interstate 170. The weather was awful, and people were poking along, but there was not much in the way of congestion.

"Have you seen a documentary called 'Invasion of the Body Snatchers'?" I asked.

"I think that's a movie, and no, I haven't seen it," she said.

"Think what you want," I said. "Perhaps life is more pleasant if you believe that aliens can't come down and snatch people."

We drove along in silence for a while.

"Do you remember when we went downtown Tuesday night?" I asked.

She said she did.

"What did you think of the traffic?" I asked.

"I don't recall there being much traffic," she said.

"Exactly," I said.

I turned on the radio. There were reports of accidents. But as one accident would be reported, there were be a report that a previous accident had been cleared.

"Cleared. That's interesting, isn't it?" I said.

Regular readers might recall some of my earlier columns about the closing of Highway 40. I anticipated disaster. In fact, I anticipated the sort of day we had Thursday. I imagined what it would be like on the alternate routes. "Think of an icy morning," I wrote. "What are we going to do when somebody slides into somebody else? People will be sitting in their cars in a line that stretches for miles. You know that somebody will be low on gas. That person won't want to shut his car off because of the cold. But if he runs out of gas, what then? How will anybody ever move?"

Just as I predicted, we had all sorts of fender-benders Thursday morning. But guess what? We did not have lines that stretched for miles. Consequently, we did not have people running out of gas.

When I wrote the columns about the horrors of the Highway 40 closing, I was not just making stuff up.

Every day I got on Highway 40 heading east from Skinker, and every day I noticed something as I had to merge into traffic. Cars. There were hundreds of them. Had I stood on an overpass and counted, I'm sure there would have been thousands. The drivers weren't joyriding, either. They were heading to work. I could tell that by the intent look that so many of them had.

All of these people were coming from the west, and when Highway 40 closed, they would have to take an alternate route. The alternate routes were going to become clogged. How could they not?

They did not become clogged. In fact, many of these alternates seem less clogged now than before the closing of Highway 40.

Something has happened to the drivers I used to see. They have disappeared. A sizable chunk of our population has simply vanished.

If they had been on the other side of the world, I might believe they had fallen

off. But they were on our side of the world. Something else happened.

I believe they have been snatched. But I didn't try to tell my daughter that. I only hinted at it.

"I remember an FBI agent who used to say, 'The truth is out there,'" I said.

"I don't think Fox Mulder was a real FBI agent," she said.

Sometimes I wish I had home-schooled her.

Bill McClellan • Gently Down the Stream

OVERWEIGHT?
NAH, JUST A HIGH BODY MASS INDEX

11.3.2006

Although I try to keep up on health issues – red wine is good – I had not heard of the body mass index until I saw a mention of it in Monday's newspaper. An 80-year-old woman wrote a letter to Lori Shontz, acting health and fitness editor, wanting to know how to calculate her body mass index.

By the way, the letter writer said she walked three miles a day but felt fatigued after each walk. My advice? Try two miles a day.

But of greater interest to me was this whole thing about the body mass index. How do you calculate it? Multiply your weight in pounds by 703, and then divide that number by the square of your height in inches.

You have to be kidding. How do scientists come up with this stuff? No wonder Republicans don't trust them. I mean, come on – 703. In your heart, you know that's a random number. That number was not the result of scientific inquiry. It isn't like Newton having an apple fall on him while he was napping after a glass or two of red wine. He awoke with a start, and then he realized: The apple had fallen down. Yes, down. Everything falls down. That observation became gravity.

That is not how we got 703. Nobody observed 703. Somebody just made it up. "Let's multiply your weight by, I don't know, 703. Ha ha ha!"

Then some other scientist came up with the notion of taking that number and dividing it by the square of your height in inches.

"We'll then call that number a body mass index, and we'll teach it in the public schools just like we teach evolution. Ha ha ha!"

Of course, we haven't even reached the tricky part. Now that we have created this bizarre number, there has to be a way to use it. So here it is: You are overweight if your body mass index is greater than 25. The letter writer said she was 5 feet 7 inches tall and weighed 163. Shontz told her that her body mass index was 25.5.

So, yes, this 80-year-old woman who walks three miles a day is overweight! What chance do the rest of us have?

I quickly calculated my own body mass index. It was 16,431. Yikes!

That had to be a mistake. Fortunately, it was. I had made what I imagine is a common error: I had taken the square root of my height in inches. Why don't the scientists just say what they mean? Take your height in inches and multiply that number by itself. When I did that, I was a more reasonable 27.8.

Not morbidly obese as much as husky. Oh, sure, I could afford to lose 10 pounds. I put the calculator back to work. If I lost 10 pounds, I would be 26.3.

What if I were at my ideal weight? I checked my drivers license. I have long maintained that a person's honesty can be measured by comparing the weight on the person's drivers license with the person's real weight. In fact, we ought to have scales in courtrooms. After a witness testifies, we could weigh the witness and then compare the real weight with the weight on the drivers license of the witness. Then the jury would have a sense of how much, well, weight to give to the testimony.

I am proud to tell you that my listed weight is within 15 pounds of my real weight. Height-wise, my listed height is within an inch of reality.

I don't know why people lie on their drivers licenses. What does it matter? When you meet somebody, you don't ask to see the person's drivers license. You just look at him. And yet, this is an essential part of our humanity. It's not just drivers licenses, either. I have checked booking sheets and have noticed that guys have clearly understated their weight and overstated their height.

Think about that. I'm talking about some rough characters who are in some serious trouble, and they still care enough to lie on their booking sheets. As if somebody will care. "He might be a criminal, but at least he has a nice body mass index."

Speaking of a nice body mass index, the guy on my drivers license is a 25.1.

HIGH HOPES FOR SON ... AND A FAMILY'S LOSS

6.29.2009

On a Monday evening in November 1999, the St. Louis University High School football team was playing Pattonville in the Missouri Class 5A quarterfinals. Pattonville was 11-0 and the area's top-ranked team. SLUH was 10-1 and ranked fifth. SLUH was ahead 14-10 at halftime, but Pattonville scored early in the second half to go ahead 17-14.

The ensuing kickoff sailed to the SLUH 6-yard line where it was caught by Willard Bryant Payne. He ran 94 yards for a touchdown. SLUH went on to win the game.

Payne had a couple of scholarship offers, but he was 5 feet 6 inches and 140 pounds, and he figured that football was not really part of his future. Not that he had any definite plans. The future was promising but vague. He was going to be, well, a professional.

That was also the viewpoint of his parents. Willard, who was known as Bryant, was the first born of Willard and Karen Payne. They had met at Southeast Missouri State University in Cape Girardeau. Willard didn't finish college, but Karen graduated with a degree in business and then went on to get an MBA at Lindenwood. She works at Boeing. Willard works in construction. They live in a middle-class neighborhood in University City.

Bryant was something of a whiz-kid in grade school. He made the honor roll every semester. He seemed to have a special knack for math and science, but when a kid gets A's in everything, it's hard to say what subject is his best. Plus, he was always athletic. He was also socially well-adjusted. An engaging kid. His parents started to dream.

Karen's dad had been a factory worker. Willard's dad was a blue-collar guy, too. So it wasn't as if either of them had come out of poverty, but still, they were thinking that their son was going to represent another step up. A doctor, a lawyer, a professional of some sort.

They decided he should go to a private high school. They are not Roman Catholic, but they heard a lot of good things about SLUH, and they were thrilled when Bryant applied and was admitted.

The academics were challenging. Bryant studied and was a B student. That was fine – a B student and a football player.

He graduated in the spring of 2000.

College was a big decision. Should he go to a traditional school or one of the historically black colleges? Karen favored the latter. How did Bryant feel about it? After four years at an all-boys school, he was just thrilled at the notion of going to a co-ed school.

So he enrolled at Florida A&M.

He did terrific his first semester. He also seemed happy. In the middle of the second semester, he went to Miami with some classmates for spring break. His parents had let him take a car to Florida. After all, he had always been responsible. He drove to Miami.

He called home during spring break. He wasn't making any sense. He was talking about his friends trying to take his car. These were kids Willard and Karen had met. Good kids. His father told him to put one of his friends on the phone. The young man said Bryant was just acting crazy.

Willard's first thought was that the boys had been drinking too much, or maybe doing drugs. We just had a couple of beers, said the young man.

Willard flew to Miami. He went to the hotel where the boys were staying. He saw his son. Something was terribly wrong. Bryant was confused. Dirty. Willard took him to the hospital. After a battery of tests, the preliminary diagnosis was paranoid schizophrenia.

Bryant dropped out of school and came home. He spent some time at a hospital. He went on medication. He went back to school in the fall, but things blew up again.

He moved back home. His mother still held to the dream that he would recover and go on to be a professional, but the bright future seemed to be sliding farther and farther away as the months turned into years. He enrolled at the University of Missouri-St. Louis, but he did not do well. He wrote music, he stayed out late, and his parents worried. One night this month, they saw him in his car with two women.

The next day, police told them his body had been found at Forest Park. The women told police Bryant had made a sexual approach toward one of them, but police told the Paynes that they believe the women took him to Forest Park to rob him.

The wake was packed. Somebody brought a photo of Bryant's teammates mobbing him after he had run back the kickoff against Pattonville. They put it up there by the coffin, a reminder of that long ago night when Willard Bryant Payne was a hero and was someday going to be a professional.

WHY ARE THESE GUYS ON CORPORATE BOARDS?

7.20.2009

My grandmother worked in a candy store after her husband abandoned her. She managed to save a little bit of money, which she put in a bank. Then the banks failed. They just closed their doors. From then on, my grandmother put her savings under her mattress.

I am more sophisticated than my grandmother – my retirement funds are invested in this and that – but I sometimes wonder if I am wiser. I wondered again last week when I read a front page story in the St. Louis Business Journal. The story was about board members who sit on the compensation committees that set executive salaries.

The story said four local men sit on two compensation committees. One of these four is Richard Liddy.

I understand there are people who can rise above failure. Look at Scott Linehan, the former coach of the Rams. He took over the Greatest Show on Turf and drove it off a cliff. In his last 20 games here, the team was 3-17. But guess what? He was offered two – two! – jobs as an offensive coordinator.

And Jim Riggleman was just hired as manager of the Washington Nationals. He has a long and consistent record of losing. In nine seasons, the three teams he managed lost 56 percent of their games. Last year, he guided the Seattle Mariners to a .400 record.

But that's sports. Managers and coaches are always being recycled.

Business is supposed to be more serious.

So my concern is not so much that Liddy is determining salaries, although that seems odd. My real concern is that he is on the boards to begin with.

He presided over one of the great wrecks in the history of St. Louis business. In 1992, he took over General American Life Insurance Co., which was then one of the bluest of the blue chips. It had billions of dollars in assets and a long history of conservative management.

Of course it had a history of conservative management. It was an insurance company. There's an old saying in the banking business, "There are no heroes in the trust department." The same thing goes with insurance companies. You take the premiums and you make safe investments. Everything is conservative, actuarial.

But in the late '90s, the market was booming. You'd go to parties and people would talk about their 401(k)s. The same thing must have been happening in the corner offices at GenAm. The fellows started thinking they were investors, not insurance men. What a shame they could invest only what they were collecting in premiums. So they went out and borrowed from money market funds and pension funds. This is called "hot money" because the lenders have the right to request repayment within seven days. GenAm did not bother to secure a line of credit in case the borrowers called in their loans.

Which they did. GenAm collapsed, was placed under state supervision and then sold to MetLife Inc.

Why would you want the guy who was responsible for that disaster giving your company advice? It's like asking Joseph Hazelwood to give you advice on shipping. He was the captain of the Valdez. He ran into Alaska. It isn't like he hit a little bitty state like Rhode Island. How can you not see Alaska?

At any rate, the Business Journal mentioned that Liddy sits on the boards of Energizer Holdings and Ralcorp Holdings. The story also noted that he was invited to be on the Ralcorp board in 2001 and that the company's proxy statement does not mention his history with GenAm.

By the way, Liddy's compensation from Ralcorp last year was $143,852. His compensation from Energizer was $175,596.

Theoretically, Liddy is not only being paid for his advice, he is watching out for the shareholders.

Who else is watching out for shareholders? Remember Robert Shapiro? He took millions from Monsanto. I once had lunch with him at his headquarters. I noticed all sorts of slogans attributed to him on the walls, and I said I felt like I was having lunch with Mao. He replied that he thought the slogans were silly, but they were good for morale. Like all these educated people feel inspired when they see these things? He is way out of touch, I thought.

Not long after he tore Monsanto apart, there was something of a scandal at the New York Stock Exchange when the public learned that NYSE Chairman Dick Grasso had a pay package of $187 million. For what? Furthermore, Grasso was on the board of Home Depot, and that company's lead director, Kenneth Langone, was also a director for the NYSE and was, in fact, the head of the compensation committee that came up with the pay package for Grasso.

In light of the bad publicity, who was named to the "reform" board? Shapiro. And who was the moralistic politician leading the charge against Grasso? That would be Eliot Spitzer.

I wonder what my grandmother would say.

PROF ENJOYS DEBATE, ROCKING THE BOAT

5.21.2010

Had Washington University professor Jonathan Katz been nominated to the Civil Rights Commission, I would understand why some people might point to his writings and object to the nomination. In particular, I would understand why his 1999 essay defending homophobia might be a cause of concern.

But he wasn't asked to join the Civil Rights Commission. He was asked to join a group of scientists working on the oil spill in the Gulf of Mexico.

What do his thoughts about sexuality have to do with that?

Nothing is the correct answer.

I should be upfront about this. I have known Katz for a long time – our kids went to grade school together – and I have always admired him. He is a man of strong opinions, and he does not care a whit if those opinions are popular.

I've written about him once. That was in 2002. Washington University had decreed that reporters needed official permission to conduct an interview on campus. According to the new guidelines, a reporter who wanted to conduct an interview on campus was required to notify the Public Affairs office, and a person from that office would have the right to monitor the interview.

So Katz called and asked if I wanted to break the rules. Of course, I said. I went to his office and interviewed him. He wanted to talk about his bosses.

"They're control freaks," he said. "This kind of policy is something you'd expect from a corporation. I have nothing against corporations, but a university is a fundamentally different thing."

He dismissed the notion of a closed campus.

"A university is a small town with public spaces open to all. There is supposed to be a free flow of ideas and people. If you don't have those things, you don't have a real university. I've done a fair amount of consulting for the defense industry, and I've seen more freedom of thought, freedom to disagree, in the defense establishment than I see here."

By the way, the door to his office was decorated with an American flag. That's unusual in the physics department. Heck, it's unusual anywhere in the university. Which is, I suspect, part of the reason he did it.

On the other hand, Katz represents something quintessentially American – a zest for engaging in the battle of ideas.

Over the years, he has often disagreed with stuff I've written. He lets me know.

His wife, Lily, is much the same. When my daughter was in fifth grade with one of the Katz kids, the class was studying Ireland. I asked a friend who had been in the Irish Republican Army to speak to the class. Lily did not share my sympathy for the IRA. But she was not against my friend speaking. She just disagreed with his views and wanted to air those differences.

There is a big difference between disagreeing with somebody and wanting to silence that person. Vigorous debate used to be considered the hallmark of a healthy democracy. We're losing our ability to engage in a debate.

Last year, opponents of health care reform went to town hall meetings not to engage in debate but to shout down speakers. There was no debate. Instead, there was chaos. That was considered a victory.

People on the left don't want to hear the other side, either. All too often, they want to ban speakers with whom they disagree. If they can't outright ban a person, they do whatever they can to show their disrespect.

Two years ago, when Phyllis Schlafly received an honorary degree at a Washington University commencement, some members of the audience stood and turned their backs toward the stage when she was introduced. I found it all very sad. We have lost the ability to respect a person with whom we disagree.

Speaking of that commencement, there was a flurry of letters to the editor concerning Schlafly's honorary degree. My favorite was from Katz.

"Some of my colleagues are upset that an honorary degree recipient disagrees with their opinions. I am more concerned (though not surprised) that the accomplishments of another recipient, the commencement speaker, seem to consist of reading headlines to a television camera," he wrote.

The speaker was Chris Matthews.

In an odd coincidence, the university is holding this year's commencement today, and the speaker is Department of Energy Secretary Steven Chu. He is the one who announced that Katz had been dismissed from the scientific group because of his social and political views.

I have no idea what Chu will talk about, but I presume it won't have anything to do with the exchange of ideas that used to be considered so vital to a free society.

SOMETHING DIDN'T ADD UP IN BOARDINGHOUSE ASSAULT

11.6.2009

Late one Saturday night in February 2008, St. Louis police Officer Timothy Ragsdale received a call that a man named Curtis Williams had reported an assault at 3945 Cook. Ragsdale went to the address and discovered that the three-story building was no longer a single-family residence but a boardinghouse.

He went room to room, but nobody acknowledged knowing a resident named Williams nor anything about an assault. Ragsdale returned to his patrol car and was about to leave when Williams walked up to the car. He had blood on his sleeves. He spoke in an agitated manner.

He said he had been in his room when a woman from a room down the hall knocked on his door and asked for a cigarette. He said he turned her down, and a few minutes later, her husband came to his door and accused him of being disrespectful.

Williams said that shortly thereafter, the husband returned with another man and they kicked his door open, entered the room and punched and kicked him. Williams said they left but returned a few minutes later with the woman and forced their way into his room again. The men attacked him, knocked him down, and the woman then grabbed his wallet and emptied it of about $260. The three left, and Williams went to a nearby liquor store to call police.

Ragsdale and Williams went back into the house, and up to the second floor where Williams lived. There were four rooms, or apartments, on the floor. All shared a common bathroom.

The door to one of the rooms was open, and Williams identified a man and woman inside as the husband and wife who had attacked him. Their names were Michael Mitchell and Jacqueline Brown-Mitchell. When Ragsdale went into the room to question the couple, he found a second man lying on his back behind the couch. His name was Eric Mingo. Williams identified him as the second attacker.

Williams later said a Sony PlayStation was missing, apparently taken when he went to the liquor store to call the police.

The three alleged assailants were charged with second-degree robbery and first-degree burglary. The two men were also charged with third-degree assault. They went to trial this week.

The defendants' version of events was outlined in an opening statement by Brad Kessler. He told the jury that Williams had a history of being rude to Brown-Mitchell. That had been the basis of the fight, which was strictly between Mitchell and Williams. Mingo, who was visiting, was passed out behind the couch, exactly where Ragsdale later found him. The robbery and the missing PlayStation were bogus accusations. Police searched the defendants and the room and found nothing.

If you are a connoisseur of the courts, you might be wondering, "How does a guy renting a room in a boardinghouse afford Brad Kessler?"

At the time of the incident, Mitchell and Mingo were working as laborers for a small remodeling company. Originally, the owner was going to pay for their legal representation, but then his business went south. He had to lay off the two and back out of the deal. But the lawyers figured they might as well see the case through. Kessler represented Mitchell. David Bruns represented Brown-Mitchell. Charles Teschner represented Mingo.

The lead prosecutor was Steven Capizzi. He was assisted by Tommy Taylor. During his days at St. Louis University's law school, Capizzi took a class in trial advocacy taught by Kessler and Bruns.

Capizzi's case depended almost entirely on Williams. Also, the state had some photographs the police had taken at the boardinghouse. The most important ones showed that the door to Williams' room had been damaged, which was consistent with his version of events.

The defense attorneys dismissed that damage. Who knows when it occurred? The boardinghouse wasn't exactly a five-star hotel. Also, the defense made much of the fact that the police hadn't found the money that was supposedly stolen, nor the PlayStation.

Finally, they attacked Williams' credibility. He had a record – domestic assault and child endangerment. He was on parole at the time of the incident. They banged away at discrepancies in his story. He told the police the second attack occurred in his room. He told the jury it occurred in the hallway.

Mitchell testified. He's 49. No convictions. He testified that Williams came to his door and complained about the noise, and that led to a fight in the hallway. He admitted punching Williams. In so doing, he was pretty much confessing to the third-degree assault, but that charge, unlike burglary and robbery, is a misdemeanor. Overall, I thought he did well.

Then again, I liked Mitchell and Mingo. "This was a 30-second drunken brawl," Mitchell told me during a break. He said he had been drinking a concoction of white wine and whiskey. He also said his life had hit the skids since getting arrested and then laid off. He said he had been sleeping in doorways and had only recently gotten into the Harbor Light. Mingo seemed like a good fellow, too. "This is all crazy," he said.

So I was hoping reasonable doubt might carry them through, but the jury, presumably swayed by the photos, found everybody guilty of everything. The verdict surprised me, and I felt bad for Mitchell and Mingo, but even as I was rooting for them, I had been wondering: If Mitchell's story were true, and Mingo was passed out behind the couch during the brief fight in the hallway, then how did Williams know to invent a second assailant?

Bill McClellan • Gently Down the Stream

WHEN IT COMES TO FAMILY, WE'RE ALL BUSINESS

4.30.2008

There was a time in this country when working people tended to stay at one company for years, and these companies – some of them, anyway – had about them the aura of a family, with the Big Boss assigned the role of benevolent father.

Dissidents used to argue that all this was nonsense, that workers had to look out for themselves. But it was comforting for people to believe in benevolence, and so this paradigm, this construction, was a part of the American workplace for years.

It was a part of this newspaper when Ernest Pulliam was hired in 1986.

He was 35. He had kicked around a little bit. He was born in St. Louis three days after Christmas in 1950. He was the sixth of 14 children. Actually, he was the final child of his parents' union. His father abandoned the family when Ernest was an infant, and his mother remarried and had eight more children with her second husband.

Ernest dropped out of Beaumont High School after his second year. He worked a series of dead-end jobs. He eventually joined the Army Reserves. After completing his six months of active duty, he returned to civilian life. He worked at a recycling center. He was laid off. He was by then a father. He did not want this wife and kids subjected to the vagaries of life with an uncertain breadwinner. He decided to improve himself. He enrolled in a program to earn his GED. This program required him to also learn a trade. He chose security. He earned his GED and completed the six-month program in security.

He was hired by a private security firm, and in January 1986, he was assigned to temporary duty at the St. Louis Post-Dispatch.

He was then, and is now, polite and friendly. He soon caught the attention of the bosses. After several months as a temporary employee, he was hired.

By the way, he was one of the workers who bought into the notion of the company as family. And why not? This has always been an informal place. A friendly person like Ernest soon knew everybody. Even Joseph Pulitzer? "Oh, yes. I saw him all the time," Ernest told me when I visited him at his home Sunday afternoon. "Mr. Pulitzer cared about people. He always had a word for you."

More family ties for Ernest. After a while, one of his daughters, Tonya, joined the newspaper as a customer service rep in the classified advertising department. In October 2004, Carolyn Olson, who worked in the features department, sent out a companywide e-mail. Her health was failing. She needed a kidney. Tonya had never met Carolyn, but she was tested and found to be a match. In January 2005, she donated a kidney to Carolyn. Both are fine today. Carolyn is retired, and Tonya is on maternity leave.

I remember talking with Ernest about his daughter's decision to donate a kidney. He was proud, of course, but he acted like it wasn't that big a deal. More of a family thing. Anybody would do it. I didn't mention that I hadn't been tested for compatibility.

Just a few days after the transplant operation, this newspaper announced the sale of Pulitzer Inc. to Lee Enterprises.

Truth is, Mr. Pulitzer had died years earlier, and the whole notion of family had been slipping away since his death. But the sale made it official. It's hard to believe in the benevolence of the Big Boss when he or she lives in a distant city.

Besides, the bottom line is the thing these days. In that regard, somebody who knows how to crunch numbers recently realized that the company could save money if we outsourced our security. So next week, we'll have a private company providing security.

"This is a difficult decision for us," explained Astrid Garcia, vice president of human resources, labor and operations at the Post-Dispatch. "This will allow us to have even more security coverage than we have now. We did ask Ernest to stay."

Ernest was invited to apply for a job with the new company, but he'd be making $10 an hour with no benefits, as opposed to the $18.77 with benefits he makes now.

There also was some talk about him getting a supervisory position with the security company, but that did not work out, and that's fine with Ernest. "I have left Egypt and I am not going back," he said. When I gave him a quizzical look, he explained that when Moses led his people out of Egypt, he told them to keep moving forward. Ernest is a member of the Lively Stone Church of God.

I'm not sure how much the newspaper will be saving. The security company has to make a profit, so it has to charge the newspaper more than its pays the guards, so we won't be saving that much on salaries. Benefits. That's where the savings are. At the moment, we have a staff of 12 in security, nine of them full time.

Health insurance is expensive, so as a shareholder, I like the savings. And as a worker, it's nice to see this whole idea of family finally put to rest.

ANYONE SELLING A BRIDGE? 'CAUSE I'VE HIT THE JACKPOT

10.16.2006

Friday was quite a day. I won the Netherlands lottery. I have never been to the Netherlands, but somehow, my e-mail account automatically registered me. My prize is a million euros.

My joy was tempered by the fact that I have twice won Spain's national lottery – El Gordo – and I have yet to see a peso. My e-mail account automatically registered me for that lottery, too. I first won that lottery a month ago, and I treated it as a joke. "It must be a scam," I thought, and I deleted the message without reading it too carefully. A couple of weeks later, I won the Spanish lottery again, and again I deleted the message.

Then I began to worry that it might be legitimate. I pictured some bureaucrat in Madrid pulling the winning number out of a bin containing thousands and thousands of such numbers. "And the winner is … Bill McClellan of St. Louis in the USA." And then one of his colleagues saying, "Didn't he win last month? Isn't he the guy who didn't respond to our e-mail?"

Perhaps I'm famous in Spain. I'm thought of as a Zen-like character, a man who doesn't care about money.

That might explain why the widow of a Nigerian oil minister keeps trying to reach me. She is living in a refugee camp. She has access to millions of dollars, but that money is in some kind of secret account, and she can't get to it from the refugee camp. She wants to do some kind of banking arrangement with me.

At first, I thought it must be a scam. Why me? Now I realize that she probably knows some people in Spain. She might have been talking to them one day and said, "I wish I knew somebody I could trust, somebody who wouldn't try to cheat me, somebody who doesn't care about money." One of the Spaniards must have said, "There is a man in St. Louis who cares nothing of money."

That would also explain another e-mail I received recently. A very wealthy Christian woman is dying of cancer, and she wants to give millions to a worthwhile cause. Would I help? Actually, I have had several such people contact me.

I thought about them on Friday. Had those people heard of me in Spain? Rich people are always running off to Europe. Now my fame will spread to the Netherlands. I imagine people will talk about me in the hashish houses in Amsterdam. "Have you heard about that righteous cat in St. Louis who doesn't care about money? He is one far-out dude."

After winning the Netherlands lottery Friday morning, I went home for lunch. While I was eating, the letter carrier came by.

One of the letters was from "The Seniors Coalition." Mary Martin, chairwoman of the board, had sent me a petition to sign. I was supposed to send it to Congress. A letter accompanied the petition and explained that U.S. and Mexican officials have decided to take Social Security money and give it to Mexicans. "In fact, the State Department plans to build an entirely new building in the U.S. Embassy complex in Mexico City just to deal with the crush of Mexican citizens expected to apply for Social Security benefits there!"

Fortunately, the Seniors Coalition has learned of this plan to give away our Social Security money. Unfortunately, the coalition is strapped for money.

"Right now, I can only afford to write to a relatively small group of loyal and concerned Americans," Chairwoman Martin explained. Why me? Perhaps she had heard that I've been winning lotteries recently.

You see, if the coalition had more money, it could get the word out. Our future could be saved.

"I hope you will dig deep and give the most generous contribution you can afford today," Chairwoman Martin wrote.

I looked for a phone number on the letter, but there wasn't one. Too bad. I was going to call the chairwoman personally and pledge a million euros to the cause. Not that I'm worried about my retirement. I don't care about those things. Ask anybody in Spain.

TWO MEN'S LIVES:
SUCCESS STORIES FROM A CHECKERED PAST

1.26.2007

R. Hal Dean was rich and famous, relatively speaking, and John Brophy was neither, but when the two died this past week, there was a certain symmetry to their passings. We've likely seen the last of their kind.

Dean went to work for Ralston Purina in 1938 as a clerk in the grain department. He had a bachelor's degree from Grinnell College in Iowa. In 1951, John Brophy went to work for the Post-Dispatch as a copy boy. He was 16 years old. His dad had died when he was 7, and his mom was struggling to raise five kids, two of whom were blind, so Brophy left high school and went to work.

Back then, St. Louis was a big-deal city, and those two institutions, Ralston and the Post, were thriving places. Locally owned, too. Both men rose in their respective organizations.

Dean became manager of the grain division, and then president of the international division and finally, in 1968, he become the CEO. It was a strange company then, almost magical. On the last day of each fiscal year, the company celebrated Checker Day. It was a daylong party. Employees wore checkered clothes. There were skits and songs. Managers ate dog food while employees cheered. The Emerald City in red and white checks.

In addition to running this unusual company – he was always an active participant in Checker Day – Dean was a civic booster. He was president of Civic Progress back when the bosses of locally owned companies really cared about St. Louis. Consider this: In 1977, when the Blues hockey team was on the verge of financial collapse, Ralston Purina stepped in and bought the team.

"Ralston Purina wouldn't have entered the hockey business if we weren't convinced that, unless we bought the team, the Blues would have left St. Louis," Dean said.

By then, Brophy had become an important cog in the newsroom at the Post-Dispatch. He had left the paper for a stint in the Army, and he came back as a clerk. He then became a reporter. He was not a stylish writer, but he was completely honest. He became an assistant city editor. In those days, the newsroom had few titled employees. The city editor had two assistants. Brophy became the chief assistant.

City editors came and went, and Brophy remained. The theory was that the world had changed and Brophy's lack of formal education was finally holding him back. He didn't seem to care. He was like the first sergeant who runs the rifle company. In fact, that's what some of the reporters called him – the first sergeant.

Dean was the last of his kind at Ralston Purina. He was replaced by William Stiritz. Frivolity had no place in the new order. Checker Day was silly. The Blues? A money loser. The team was sold. In fact, other bits and pieces of the company were sold, and then finally, the company itself was swallowed by Nestle.

In 1992, the bosses at the newspaper offered Brophy a title: assistant managing editor for administration. He turned down the title but took the job and became the newsroom administrator. If anybody wanted anything, they went to Brophy. He had been unflappable as an assistant city editor, and he continued to be a calming presence as newsroom administrator.

There have always been a few prima donnas at the newspaper – they're tolerated if not admired – and sometimes their requests were off the wall. I remember when one prima donna complained that he deserved to sit near a window. He was tired of looking at the wall. Brophy listened patiently, and when I came in the next day, an illuminated scene of a waterfall was hanging on the wall next to my desk. It was from a saloon.

Brophy retired in 1999. He died Saturday. He was 71. Dean died Monday in Scottsdale, Ariz. He was 90.

Checker Days and a high school dropout running a newsroom. Could either happen today?

EVICTION NOTICE ADDS TO PLIGHT OF TRANSGENDER COUNTY RESIDENT

8.23.2006

When Beverly first moved into the apartment complex in south St. Louis County 25 years ago, she was a man, and she was called Gary. She was, even then, a little odd. For instance, she painted her toenails. She sometimes wore lipstick.

But that sort of thing can be ignored. When she started wearing dresses, the situation became harder to ignore. Maybe impossible. In addition to being a very large person – she stands 6 feet 1 and weights 366 pounds – Beverly has a man's deep voice and she talks like, well, a man.

"I sometimes shoot my mouth off," she told me.

She is, she said, transgender, a woman trapped in a man's body.

That would be a difficult road for even an effeminate man, but for a person like Beverly, it has to be especially rough. She is trapped in a body that does not easily translate into womanhood. Nor does she have much of a chance for surgery.

"I'm classified as morbidly obese," she said. "I'd have to lose more than 150 pounds to qualify as a candidate for surgery, and then I'd need money. No way. Even in Thailand, it's supposed to be about $11,000."

Speaking of Thailand, wasn't John Mark Karr, the latest suspect in the murder of JonBenet Ramsey, trying to get a sex change operation over there? Beverly sighed. The general public already is dubious about transgender people. Now this.

Actually, Beverly's problems are more prosaic. She recently received an eviction notice. A section of the lease was cited: "Neither tenant nor any person on premises with his permission shall disturb, annoy, inconvenience or endanger neighbors." Beverly stands accused of annoying and disturbing people. Something about an argument. Another tenant alleged that Beverly threatened him. Beverly said there was a quarrel, but some of her remarks were misconstrued. I called the number on the eviction notice. "We're sorry. Due to network difficulties, your call cannot be completed," a voice said.

Perhaps Beverly's counselor at BJC HealthCare can find her a place. He did not return my phone calls.

Fortunately, there is some time. Beverly has until the end of October to vacate her apartment.

Perhaps her church can find her a place. Beverly attends church regularly. I called her pastor. The pastor said she could not say anything about Beverly. Confidentiality, she said. In fact, she said, she would prefer the church not be mentioned in any article about Beverly.

I asked Beverly about her early days.

She is 53 years old. She said she was raised in south St. Louis and graduated from Cleveland High School. She said her dad was a rough-and-tumble sort of guy. She started in that direction herself, she said, but she never felt really comfortable in that role. She had three older sisters, and she liked wearing their dresses. She was not sexually attracted to men – she still isn't – and her confusion about gender identity led to a bunch of problems. She said she was misdiagnosed as a schizophrenic and spent 16 months at St. Louis State Hospital on Arsenal Street.

She receives disability payments, food stamps and gets housing assistance. She showed me a tray of medicines, and she said she has diabetes, glaucoma, high blood pressure and gout.

She has shoulder-length brown hair. She was wearing jeans and a blouse when I visited. Her toenails were painted pink. "I look like a hybrid today," she said. Her apartment is small and cluttered. Compact discs and records are stacked everywhere. She said she mostly sits around and listens to music. "My life is what you see here," she said.

What about a social life? Do women find her appealing when she dresses as a woman? No, but then again, they didn't find her appealing before, either, she said.

She worries about finding another place, but she figures things will work out. "I'm emotionally distressed right now, but I have always been a lucky person," she said.

A WARTIME LOVE LOST, BUT NEVER FORGOTTEN

5.28.2007

In the spring of 1944, as Frannie Dolan was finishing her junior year in high school, she met Francis Xavier Kelly. He was in training at Scott Air Force Base with one of Frannie's neighbors, so she got fixed up with him. They went to the Powhatten Theater in Maplewood and then to the Priscella Shop for a soda. They did this several times during the summer before he was sent overseas. They exchanged letters through the fall, winter and into the spring.

Then Kelly's parents called. His plane had gone down over Germany. After the war, the bodies of the crew members were brought to Jefferson Barracks National Cemetery for a mass burial. Frannie attended the service.

Decades passed.

Two years ago, Fran Noonan, the former Frannie Dolan, was at Jefferson Barracks National Cemetery for a Memorial Day service. She decided to visit Kelly's grave site. She found fresh flowers and a note. "My dear love Bart, I miss you very much. Love you with all my heart forever." Fran was puzzled. She looked at the names on the common stone: Frances F. Golubski, Aram G. Kadehjian, Francis J. Kelly, Jr., Horace B. Lane, Joseph H. Mull, Jr., Irving Smarinsky.

Last year, Fran visited the grave site again. There were more flowers and another note. "Bart sweetheart. I think of you so much and I love you forever. Your devoted Marian."

Fran went to the florist. He took her name and number and said he'd give them to the woman who had sent the flowers. Later that day, Marian Love called.

Marian grew up in a small town in Iowa. When she finished her junior year of high school in the spring of 1944, she went to California to spend the summer with her brother and his wife. Her brother was in the Army Air Forces and stationed at March Field near Riverside. Marian got a job on the base as a typist. After work, she would swim at the officers' pool.

That is where she met Horace Bartlett Lane. He was 21 years old. He had grown up in Seattle. He had started college at Washington State University. He was majoring in chemical engineering, but dropped out to enlist. He wanted to be a pilot. He saw Marian in the pool and offered to give her swimming lessons. He was very polite, very serious.

Several days later, he asked her to dinner. They began seeing each other every day. He was waiting for an assignment to a B-24. He would then be headed to the war in Europe. In late August, he was assigned to a crew. He would be leaving in a matter of weeks.

Marian and Bart had been telling each other that they were engaged to be engaged, but now with his departure imminent, Bart gave her a ring. But when to get married? After the war? Marian wrote her parents. I want to get married now, she said. Her parents initially balked, but then agreed. How could you pretend things were normal in the midst of the war?

They were married on Sept. 8 in a small church on base and then went to Los Angeles for a two-day honeymoon. A few nights before he left, he was stretched out on the bed. He told Marian that he had been offered a training position but had turned it down because he wanted to stay with his crew and do his part. Now he regretted the decision. He looked terribly sad.

On Oct. 6, he left. Marian returned to Iowa and went back to high school.

She wrote her husband every day. Long letters, always upbeat, never mentioning the fear that ate at her.

In early March, his letters stopped. On March 20, she received a telegram. He was missing.

On March 3, the formation of B-24 bombers crossed the English Channel and was about 40 miles north of its target of Madgeburg, Germany, when the Messerschmidts attacked. One of the bombers was hit and fell into the B-24 that Bart was co-piloting. A gunner and bombardier managed to bail out. They were later captured and eventually released. The others went down with the plane. Among them was the radio operator, Francis Xavier Kelly.

Of the 19 members of the two planes, three survived. The others were buried in a common grave in Madgeburg.

Marian graduated from high school and moved to Seattle to be with Bart's parents while they awaited his return. The war ended, and there was no word of Bart. Marian enrolled at the University of Washington. In March 1946, a year after he had been reported missing, Bart was declared dead. Marian was a widow. She had just turned 19.

Her father suggested she get a new start. She enrolled at the University of Colorado. At a Halloween dance, she met a tall, serious-looking young man. His name was Bill Love. He was working on his master's degree in engineering. He had been in the Navy during the war, assigned to submarines. His training had ended just as the war had.

Marian and Bill were married in August 1947.

They spent some time in California and then they went to the University of Illinois, where Bill received a Ph.D. in mechanical engineering in 1952. By then, they had three daughters.

Also by then, Bart's remains were at Jefferson Barracks National Cemetery. The remains had been recovered from the common grave at Madgeburg, and eventually, all but six had been individually identified. The remains of those six were reinterred in 1949 at Jefferson Barracks in a common grave.

While the Loves lived in Illinois, they visited the grave site.

Marian was honest with Bill. She had periodic bouts of almost inconsolable grief. He would comfort her during these periods.

In 1970, Bill got a job as a professor at the University of Washington. By that time, Bart's father had died, but his mother was still living, and Marian and Bill would visit. Bill always hugged her. She said she loved him.

Marian always thought the two men were alike. Tall, smart, kind and serious. Both had an aptitude for engineering. Even their names – Lane and Love.

In 1992, Marian and Bill took a trip to England to see the airfield where Bart had been stationed.

Still, it would be wrong to think that Marian was living in the past. She loved Bill. She loved their family. She just didn't want Bart to be forgotten.

Bill always said he understood. Marian let him read the letters Bart had sent her. This is the sort of man I'd want a daughter to marry, Bill said. By the way, the children – two sons followed the three daughters – always knew about Bart.

Bill died in January. Marian had him cremated. When she dies, she will be cremated and their ashes will be buried together.

In the meantime, she sends flowers to Bart.

TWO ILL MEN'S PATHS CROSS ON S. GRAND

3.7.2010

Henry Kotyla was a street character, and the street was South Grand Boulevard. He was part of the fabric of that vibrant street, laughing and talking and waving at people. He was a strange sort of man, but he was friendly and happy and nobody thought of him as dangerous or threatening.

He was a paranoid schizophrenic.

His sister, Janis Ramsey-Melton, took care of him. She made sure that he had food in his apartment and that his bills were paid.

She said her brother was once normal, and that he was married and had children, but long ago he was the victim of an armed robbery while working at a gas station. She thinks the trauma of that event sent him into a downward spiral. Who knows?

Randolph Stevens lived just off South Grand on Giles Avenue. He was almost as reclusive as Kotyla was outgoing. Steve Meyer lived on the first floor of the four-family flat in which Stevens lived on the second floor, and Meyer, who is outgoing himself, did not even know Stevens' first name.

He thought it was Mike, and so he'd greet him that way. "Hey, Mike. How you doing?"

Then one day Stevens said to him, "I AM NOT MIKE!"

People were scared of Stevens.

He was a paranoid schizophrenic.

Dr. P. Lynn Wakefield, a psychiatrist who treated Stevens almost 20 years ago at the John Cochran VA Medical Center and helped him get on Social Security disability, said his experiences in Vietnam with the 101st Airborne in 1968-69 might have contributed to his condition. Who knows?

On a Saturday night in April 2006, Kotyla came to the apartment on Giles to visit Meyer, a longtime friend. But Meyer was in the shower, and his girlfriend told Kotyla to come back later.

Shortly thereafter, Kotyla was shot to death on South Grand. A witness identified Stevens as the shooter. Police went to his apartment. He told them he had been on his way to the store when he ran into Kotyla and shot him during an argument.

Others questioned that story. Meyer thought Stevens had followed Kotyla. "He didn't like Henry. He used to say he could hear him walking blocks away."

Sadly, we live in a time when shootings are not uncommon, and when a 58-year-old man with a mental condition shoots a 52-year-old man with a mental condition, the case hardly merits a mention in the newspaper.

The only reason this case rated even a small story was the fact that Stevens had a concealed-carry permit. At the time of the shooting, a reporter quoted a homicide detective who said that this was the first instance in St. Louis in which a man accused of murder had a concealed-carry permit for the alleged murder weapon.

The permit was from Florida, and the story noted that once Missouri's concealed-carry law was passed, it became common for residents to obtain permits from states that offered reciprocity but did not require residency.

That way, applicants could take advantage of the Missouri law more quickly, especially since St. Louis and St. Louis County were slow to implement the permit provisions.

The story did not mention that Stevens had a history of mental illness.

He went to trial in December and was convicted of second-degree murder. He was sentenced on Friday.

Circuit Court Judge Lisa Van Amburg asked if anybody wanted to address the court before she pronounced sentence.

Ramsey-Melton talked about the joy that her brother brought to the world. Meyer spoke in the same vein. Two firefighters from the station at Potomac Street and Grand Boulevard said that Kotyla would cheer everybody up when he visited.

Assistant Circuit Attorney Tanja Engelhardt said the state recommended a life sentence. The community needs to be protected, she said.

Van Amburg asked Stevens if he had anything to say. He was wearing bright orange garb from the city jail. His gray hair was disheveled. He began to speak in an agitated manner. He waved his hands. He said something about Hamlet. His attorney, public defender Edward Scott Thompson, tried to soothe him, but to no effect.

Van Amburg said the reference to Hamlet was appropriate.

She said this case, like the play, was a tragedy. She said it was a tragedy that the Department of Corrections has become the main provider of treatment for mental illnesses, and she said it is a tragedy that a person with a mental illness can get a concealed-carry permit.

She then sentenced Stevens to 15 years in prison. He is 61.

Bill McClellan • Gently Down the Stream

FOR PIANO TUNER, IT'S THE BUSIEST TIME OF THE YEAR

11.28.2008

Charles Merkel is a piano tuner. This is the busiest time of the year for him. There is a timelessness to that, I said, and I mentioned something about people standing around a piano singing Christmas carols. Merkel shook his head. A piano is a wooden acoustic instrument, and it is affected by humidity, he said matter of factly. The air is drier in the winter. That's why they need tuning now, he explained.

Lest you think there is no room for sentimentality in his world of piano tuning, you should know that this is more than a job to Merkel. He is the fifth generation of his family to make a living in the piano business. He is called Charles, but his real name is Louis Charles Merkel III. He is the great-great-grandson of the first Louis Charles Merkel, who arrived in this country from Germany in 1849.

He was one of two piano makers from the same area of Lower Saxony to arrive in this country about that time. Almost certainly they knew each other. Both found piano-making jobs in New York. Merkel stayed in that city for about 10 years and then moved to St. Louis where he started his own piano factory. The other stayed in New York and established his factory there. His name was Henry Steinway.

One can look back on that now and say that Steinway made the right decision, but at the time, St. Louis must have seemed a perfect market. Wealthy planters in the antebellum South could afford the very best, and Merkel pianos were soon being carried down the Mississippi to the great plantations. Some stayed here, of course. An example of a Merkel piano can be seen at the Chatillon-DeMenil Mansion in Benton Park.

The Civil War and the demise of the great planters did not seem to hurt Merkel's business. Perhaps that's because the city was growing. Several years after the war, Merkel moved his factory from around Park and South Broadway to the present site of the Busch Stadium East Parking Garage. The factory burnt in 1885. Shortly thereafter, Merkel died.

The second Louis Charles Merkel remained in the piano business, but he was a salesman rather than a piano maker. He also received a patent for making uprights sound more like grands. Mostly, though, he was a piano tuner.

His son, Clarence James Merkel, stayed in the piano business, but sometimes barely so. The Great Depression was not a good time for pianos. The business shrank to almost nothing, and according to family lore, Clarence kept things going by making and selling bootleg liquor. He would later tell his grandchildren about paying off the local sergeant: "That was how we stayed, if not on the right side of the law, on the ignored side."

Still, he loved pianos, and he married Loretta Burns, who worked in the piano department of Famous-Barr. Their son, Louis James Merkel, stayed in the piano business. He restored old pianos and he tuned pianos, but mostly, he sold them. He had a thriving store on Big Bend and then he moved to a location in the Warson Village Shopping Center. His store was one of the first in the country to sell the Yamaha brand.

He and his wife, Donna, had a daughter and two sons – Lois, Charles and Jim – and for a while, it seemed that none of them would stay with pianos. Lois was an artist and later went to law school. Charles studied economics, sociology and philosophy in college. Jim went to journalism school.

But after graduating from college and traveling around the world, Charles was unsure what to do with his life.

"Why don't I show you how to tune?" said his father. That was in 1974. Charles has been tuning ever since.

He has a list of about 1,200 clients. About 500 of them are regulars. On a good day, he might tune five pianos. He generally works six days a week. He never married, and his hobby is traveling. He works nine months a year and travels three. He has visited 130 countries, and he has tuned pianos on every continent except Antarctica.

Exactly how does one tune a piano?

We were at Jim's house when I asked the question. Jim is the family historian. He's a reporter and covers south St. Louis and City Hall for the Suburban Journals. He also has a piano. (His wife, Lorraine, plays.) Charles went to the piano and lifted off the front, exposing the wires that are stretched over a sounding board.

"There are two ways to do this," he said. "I'll show you the way I was trained."

He touched a tuning fork to the wood, and then took a wrench – called a tuning hammer – and began to tighten one of the wires, getting the middle key of A to duplicate the pitch of the tuning fork. He was soon hitting other keys and stretching other wires, listening intently. Clearly, this was as much art as science. Then he said, "Here is the new way." He took a small computer out of his bag and put it on the piano. It seemed to operate like a carpenter's level. Instead of adjusting the wires by ear, a tuner simply watches the computer.

"It's as if you don't have to even listen," I said.

"Most tuners wear ear plugs these days," said Charles.

Maybe he could read the dismay in my face. No art to it at all?

"I don't wear ear plugs," he said.

Of course, he doesn't. He might be called Charles, but he is really Louis Charles Merkel III.

CHILD PORN ENSNARES ADOPTER OF CHILDREN

7.3.2009

Charles Murray taught physics at Francis Howell North High School. He was also head of the science department. His wife, Johnna, had a master's degree in accounting and was a certified public accountant. They had a home in St. Charles.

They were unable to have children and decided to adopt. In 2001, they went to Romania and adopted an 11-month-old boy. In 2004, they went to Russia to adopt a 15-month-old boy. While they were at the orphanage, they saw a 5-year-old girl. She had cerebral palsy. They decided to adopt her, too.

On July 9 of 2007, Charles and Johnna celebrated the 25th anniversary of their first date. He gave her a dozen roses. Life seemed challenging, but full.

Two days later, shortly after Johnna left for work, police and federal agents came to the house. They had information that Charles had child pornography on his computer.

He did.

He had a secret life. He spent hours on the computer in the basement looking at pornography. He collected the stuff. He traded pornography with people on the Internet. Although almost all of the images were of adults – seamy stuff but legal – some were of children.

Murray's secret life went agley when authorities traced images from a computer in Ohio to a computer in Missouri. The Missouri man's online name was Uncle Chester. That was Murray.

He was soon indicted. He contacted a lawyer, who was honest with him. "You will go to prison." Charles and Johnna sold their home and moved to a house near Charles' parents so Johnna could get help with the three kids. They heard through the grapevine that the rumor in their old neighborhood was that Murray had been busted for meth. After all, he was a science teacher. The Murrays heard that rumor and felt something akin to relief. Meth sounds better than child porn.

And yet, while they didn't want to seem to be minimizing the evils of child pornography, they couldn't help but feel that he was guilty of no more than being addicted to porn.

"I'm glad it's over," Murray told me when we first spoke several months ago. "I don't mean I'm glad about going to prison, but I'm glad it's over."

He insisted he was not a pedophile. He said he was in therapy and was dealing with his addiction. He said he had thrown out a collection of Playboys.

Shortly after we first spoke, he pleaded guilty on one count of receiving child pornography. He went to court Monday for sentencing.

The day before, this newspaper ran a story about a man in O'Fallon who had several "hot tub parties" with three girls – two were 15, one was 16 – and gave them pot and booze and allegedly touched one of the girls inappropriately. Police were notified and they seized the man's computer. When no child pornography was found, the case languished and eventually fell through the cracks.

It's as if looking at pictures is worse than actually doing something.

The mandatory minimum for receiving child pornography is 60 months in prison.

Still, the defense made an effort. Murray's counselor took the stand and testified that Murray was a motivated patient and did not fit the profile of a pedophile. He had a compulsion disorder, the counselor said.

In cross-examination, assistant U.S. Attorney Reggie Harris asked, "Have you seen the images?"

"I have not," said the counselor. Me neither, I admitted to myself.

Murray cried when he addressed the court. "I am so glad it's over. I am so glad it's over," he said.

U.S. District Court Judge Henry Autry then pronounced sentence. I remember once watching him have a lunch of yogurt and cigarettes, and I realized then that he is a man who understands the complexities of life. He no longer smokes, but still, I found myself wishing that he had some latitude in this case.

Actually, there was no indication that he would have been lenient. His major decision had to do with the length of time Murray will spend on supervised release when he gets out of prison. The defense was asking for no more than five years. Autry's decision – lifetime supervision.

So that was it – 60 months in prison and lifetime supervision.

Autry also ruled that Murray could go home for now. He will be notified when to report for prison.

Murray's children were waiting in the hallway outside of the courtroom. He hugged them, and they hugged him, and then the family headed toward the elevators.

Bill McClellan • Gently Down the Stream

SEASONS FLY BY IN THE BLINK OF AN EYE

9.7.2008

The rain stopped Thursday night, and Friday morning it was autumn. There was nothing gradual about the change in seasons.

Of course, it had been obvious for a while that fall was coming. Even before Labor Day, children had started going past my house each morning on their way to school. Sometimes I'd be outside and I'd chat with the parents as they walked past. I can usually be called upon to say something trite. "It goes by in the blink of an eye," is one of my standards.

When we moved into our house, my wife was pregnant with our first child. As the years went by, older neighbors, whose kids already were gone, would say similar things to me. Now most of those older neighbors are gone, replaced by the young parents who go past my house. It is easy for a sentimental person to get morose as the seasons change.

On Friday morning, I saw a monarch butterfly in our backyard. Now if ever a creature had reason to be morose at the coming of fall, it's a monarch butterfly.

Monarch butterflies fly to the mountains of Michoacán in central Mexico for the winter. Imagine that. A monarch butterfly weighs about an ounce. What happens if it hits a headwind? A goose is big enough to just plow through a headwind, but a butterfly? Yet they come from as far north as Canada into the Mexican mountains. That's about a 2,500-mile trip.

What's more, it's an intergenerational trip. The butterflies that winter in Mexico never have been there before. They are the descendants of butterflies who spent the previous winter in the mountains. Yet scientists think they not only return to the same few groves, but maybe even the same trees as did their relatives. They hang from the oyamel fir trees in huge bunches. They mate in the groves. The males then die, and the females make it north to the U.S. Gulf of Mexico states before laying eggs and dying themselves.

I decided to see the butterflies for myself last year. My family and I were in Texas visiting relatives at Christmas. My daughter had to get back to California where she teaches high school biology. My wife had to get back to St. Louis for work. My son was on winter break from the University of Wisconsin and still had about a week before he had to be back at school. Let's go to Mexico, I said. Maybe we can see the butterflies in Michoacán.

Jack and I flew to Mexico City at night and turned around the next morning and caught a flight north to Zacatecas, which is the northernmost of the silver cities. We stayed there for two days. We went to a wonderful saloon called Las Quince Letras – the Fifteen Letters – and met Alfonso Lopez Monriel. I was wearing a cap from the city of Derry in Northern Ireland. Alfonso told us he had been in Northern Ireland during the Troubles. Which side were you on? I asked. "I am an atheist," he said, "but a Catholic one."

Jack and I took a nine-hour bus ride to Morelia, the capital of Michoacán. We tried to catch a bus to Angangueo, the closest town to the most famous of the butterfly reserves, El Rosario. But the road was out, and we ended up in Zitácuaro, which is the city closest to the most recently opened reserve, Cerro Pellón.

The entrance to the reserve is next to a cluster of houses. The man at the gate asked if we wanted to rent horses. How long a hike is it? we asked. About two hours, he said. We chose to hike. You'll need a guide, he said, and he called over to a young man from the cluster of houses.

Did I say a young man? I should have said a mountain goat. He led us up a footpath that sometimes disappeared. I became exhausted. Up and up we went. Finally, we reached a clearing. There were monarch butterflies. Not as many as I had hoped for, but lots of them. It was a bit like being in a butterfly house at a zoo.

Perfect, I said, and collapsed.

No, a little farther, said our guide.

We went around the bend. Thousands and thousands of monarch butterflies were hanging from the fir trees like living ornaments. Butterflies were joining the clumps and leaving the clumps. They were flying around. They were all over.

It was a spectacular sight, but a little sad, too. The males would not make it out of the grove. The females would not make it all the way home.

I thought about that as I saw the butterfly in my yard. "It goes by in the blink of an eye," I said to him.

Bill McClellan • Gently Down the Stream

THE EVOLUTION OF NEWSPAPERS CAN BE TRACED TO TWO METEORS

9.28.2007

The barosaurus did not see the meteor hit. That's because he was at a watering hole on Tucker Boulevard. But even from inside the saloon, he could hear it. Kaboom! It was like thunder. The glasses on the bar shook. A little beer slopped out of the glass that the bartender had put in front of the barosaurus.

"Hey, Athena. I ought to get a free beer," said the barosaurus. "Hahaha."

Later, the barosaurus went back to the newspaper. From a fifth-floor window, he could not see the actual point of impact, but a dust cloud was visible, rising slowly just this side of the horizon.

"What was that?" the barosaurus asked a colleague.

"Something called the Internet," the colleague said.

Actually, it didn't happen quite that way. There was no explosion. I can't even remember when I first heard of the Internet, and when I did hear of it, I didn't realize it would change the world of newspapering. A friend who is smarter about these things tried to warn me.

"This has the potential of hurting classified ad sales," he said.

"Not everybody has a computer," I said.

"You don't understand business," he said. "If you and I have a store and somebody opens a similar store down the street, he doesn't have to take 100 percent of our business to hurt us. He can cut into our margins."

Margins?

I do remember when the second meteor hit. Public ownership. One day in the late 1980s, a businessman from Michigan announced his intention to buy the Pulitzer Publishing Co., or at least part of it.

At the time, the company was wholly owned by the descendants of the first Joseph Pulitzer. There was nothing unusual about that. Most newspapers were family-owned.

With the benefit of hindsight, I can see that was a wonderful thing. Owning a newspaper wasn't as cool as owning a sports team, but it was more fun than owning a widget factory. The families that owned the newspapers were generally wealthy, and as long as their newspapers weren't losing money, the families were happy.

But the implications of all of that were lost on me at the time. In fact, I had fun with the notion of a businessman from Michigan trying to buy the paper. Among his other holdings was A&W Root Beer, and I wrote a column about the good feelings I had about an A&W Root Beer stand near my childhood home. "I recommend the chili dog basket," I wrote.

Some of the descendants of the original Joseph Pulitzer wanted to sell, and the other members decided to buy them out, and the best way to raise the necessary cash was to go public. The same scenario was playing out in other cities around the country.

Newspapers became public properties. Wealthy families might not have cared much about profits, but stockholders did. So newspapers became more efficient, less wasteful.

That might sound like a good thing. What's wrong with a little efficiency? But some things are simply counterintuitive.

Drinking at lunch, for instance. In the days of the three-martini lunch, American business was the envy of the world. Now hardly anybody drinks at lunch, and we're a debtor nation. Is there a connection? I don't know. Back when newspapers were less efficient, they were better. More interesting, fewer errors – just better.

All of this comes to mind because today is another momentous day at the newspaper. It is the final day of work for 60 of my colleagues in the newsroom and other various departments. They've taken a buyout. A few will retire. Most will go on to other ventures. Some of them are people whose names are familiar to regular readers. Others worked behind the scenes. All will be missed.

It's worth noting that these buyouts are not unique to this newspaper. They're happening all around the country. It's a good way to cut costs. A leaner newspaper is a more efficient newspaper. Also, a lot of the younger people are more computer savvy. They understand interactive media. It's the coming thing.

The barosaurus thinks of these interactive media people as mammals. They are made for this new world. Meanwhile, the barosaurus often stares out the fifth-floor window. He tries to remember the day before the meteor hit.

DEATH, CRIME MARK SHIFT IN SMALL TOWN

6.12.2009

Kenneth Hartman Sr. died at the age of 72 from cirrhosis of the liver. He never drank. He was born and reared on a family farm near Waterloo. For many years, he served as director of the Monroe County Fair Association, which featured, among other things, demolition derbies and tractor pulls.

He used his own tractor to level the track for those events. "He could run that tractor forwards and backwards," said his wife of 50 years.

That is a nice way to be remembered.

Hartman's death made the front page of last week's Republic-Times, a weekly newspaper in Monroe County. I came across the story when I went to Waterloo on Wednesday for Christopher Coleman's preliminary hearing. Coleman is charged with murdering his wife, Sheri, and their two young sons in Columbia.

It seemed a little disconcerting to read about Hartman and then sit through Coleman's hearing. I do not mean to suggest that Waterloo is Mayberry. Maybe it once was, but that would have been long ago. These days, people in small towns are as sophisticated as their big-city counterparts.

That was evident at the preliminary hearing, when Columbia Police Chief Joe Edwards testified. He was very professional, very matter of fact. He was out of "Law & Order" rather than "Andy Griffith." He laid out part of the state's case against Coleman.

The state is not required to show its entire hand at a preliminary hearing. There is no need to prove a defendant guilty beyond a reasonable doubt. There is only the need to show probable cause to have a trial.

Published reports had already indicated that Coleman had a girlfriend, that medical tests showed his wife and sons were dead before he said he left the house for an early morning workout, that police had found some things connected to the murders – a glove, twine – along the route from his house to the gym.

Actually, that stuff would have been sufficient for a preliminary hearing.

But Edwards had new information. He said experts had linked certain threatening notes to Coleman's laptop computer.

If you've followed this case, you know that long before the murders, Coleman had reported receiving threatening notes that supposedly had to do with his job as security manager for televangelist Joyce Meyer.

That seemed plausible, or at least possible. After all, Meyer makes her livelihood in a rather odd fashion. She asks people to send her money, and many people do. What does she offer in return? Redemption. Grace. An opportunity to be close to God.

But some people want to be close to Meyer, and that is not practical. She cannot be close to everybody who sends her money.

Some of those people get disenchanted.

Among Coleman's duties were keeping the disenchanted away from Meyer.

So those notes represented an alternative to the state's theory. If you're thinking like a defense attorney, you're thinking that people who send money to a person they don't know in return for something as nebulous as grace are slightly out of kilter. At least some of them might be. Hey, it's an argument.

But if the state could show that Coleman wrote the threatening notes himself, the state not only takes away that alternate theory, it adds a stronger element of premeditation. I can imagine a prosecutor's closing argument. "He set this up long before he did it. Even as his little boys kissed him good night and told him they loved him, he was planning to do this."

I sat a couple of rows behind Coleman's family and I was unable to see their reaction to Edwards' testimony. Later, they chose not to speak with reporters.

Coleman sat through the testimony without expression. In person, he appears smaller, less fleshy, than he does in photographs. A nice-looking young man, actually, who had a beautiful family – and seemingly a happy one.

"Sheri never said anything to me," said her cousin, Enrico Mirabelli, "and I'm the divorce lawyer in the family." Mirabelli had come in from Chicago.

Mirabelli and other members of Sheri's family shared the front row with Coleman's family. Reporters and other spectators filled the rest of the courtroom.

By the way, I sat next to Corey Saathoff, the Republic-Times reporter who did such a nice job on the Hartman story. Cirrhosis of the liver and he never drank. That's life, though. Even the nice stories can be inexplicable.

'LIEUTENANT BLUES' ALWAYS SEEMED TO FIND HIS MAN

11.23.2008

Charlie O'Brien was a lieutenant in the St. Louis police department when he retired in 1983.

"He was the nicest man you ever met," said Jerry Leyshock, who is now a captain. "He was a gentleman. A gentle man. He was old school. I remember him at homicide and shooting scenes. Always very calm."

For years, he had been a detective. His son, Mark, remembers him standing on the sidelines at soccer games wearing a fedora and a trench coat. He could have come from Central Casting. In fact, there's a photo from the 1950s when he had a secondary job working security at the Fox. He's posing with Debbie Reynolds. She's smiling at him and he's grinning at the camera. He's wearing his fedora. He looks like James Cagney.

He mostly worked burglary and robbery, and he was good at his job, but his hobby earned him legendary status and the nickname, the Hunter.

In the '50s and '60s, he looked for old-time blues musicians. He was especially interested in the ones who had recorded in the '20s, when St. Louis had a vibrant blues scene. It was then strictly black music, and the venues were strictly black ones, and the musicians who played on the streets and in the speakeasies and bars in the '20s had 30 years later melted back into the black community in a segregated city.

O'Brien went into their world to look for them. He'd go into pool halls and bars. A white guy with a trench coat and a fedora had no need to identity himself as a cop. "I'm looking for a guy named Rufus," he might say. "He's an albino. Maybe you know him as Red." That was one of the first guys he found – Rufus Perryman, better known as Speckled Red. O'Brien found Perryman in 1954. His search had come up empty, and then one day he answered a call for a disturbance at a pool hall, and the man doing the disturbing was an albino of about the right age. It was Perryman.

O'Brien introduced him to Bob Koester, another blues aficionado who had started a recording label, Delmark. Perryman made a couple of recordings and resumed his career.

Henry Brown was another find. In the days before the lottery, there was something called the numbers game, or the policy. Brown, an old-time piano player, was a policy manager, and when he heard there was a white cop asking about him, he was in no mood to be found.

"Charlie finally found him and knocked on his apartment door," said Kevin Belford, who is writing a book about the history of the blues in St. Louis. "The door opened a tiny bit and then closed. 'I'm not here about the numbers. I'm here about your music,' Charlie said, and then the door opened again."

Like Perryman, Brown resumed his career. O'Brien found Walter Davis working at a switchboard in a hotel. He found Harmonica Sam Fowler at a shoeshine parlor. He found Big Joe Williams, Jelly Jaw Short and Barrelhouse Buck McFarland, who proved who he was by banging out a tune on a piano at the Pinkie Boxx Hair Salon, and later wrote a song about O'Brien – "Lieutenant Blues."

If you want to see the musicians O'Brien found, many of their pictures can be found above the bar at BB's Jazz Blues & Soups on South Broadway.

O'Brien died in January. I thought about him this month when his son, Kelty O'Brien, was murdered. He was shot to death in his pickup in the Tower Grove South neighborhood.

Kelty O'Brien was a large man, 6-2, 240. He was much bigger than his father. More flamboyant, too. If you see a group photo with Kelty in it, he will be in the middle. He was always a star. He was the captain of the soccer team at St. Louis University High School in 1981. He organized softball teams. He was always the best hitter. He was murdered the day before his 46th birthday.

Kelty was the youngest of three brothers. The oldest, Brady, was murdered in 1990. He was stabbed to death. He had been at the racetrack, later at a White Castle. Maybe he had a bundle of money and somebody saw it when he paid for his burgers. Maybe it was a street robbery. Or a fight. Who knows? The murder was never solved.

Brady's murder was not the first such tragedy in Charlie O'Brien's life. His mother, Lucille, was murdered in her apartment in June 1952. She had left the door open because of the heat. A prowler shot her. She lived just long enough to tell a neighbor she didn't know her assailant. It had to have hit the lieutenant hard. He never knew his father. Lucille's murder was never solved.

Now Kelty. Three murders in one family. I called the surviving brother, Mark. (There are also three sisters, two from the lieutenant's second marriage.) Mark is a St. Louis police officer. He joined the department in 1979, quit in 1986 to go into the billiard parlor business, and returned in 2005. I mentioned that the first two murders were unsolved. He said he had a lot of faith in the homicide unit.

I called Capt. Jim Gieseke. He said he had not known the lieutenant, but knew of him. I asked if he thought Kelty's murder was a random crime.

"We don't believe it was random," he said. "We believe somebody intended to kill him. We're trying to piece this together. The 'whys' we don't know yet. Without getting too deep into it, the surveillance cameras from the company across the street have been helpful."

Kelty used to hang out at Shanti's in Soulard. A benefit to help pay his funeral expenses will be held at the saloon next Saturday night. Any extra money will be donated to BackStoppers. Devin Allman will perform. He's the son of Gregg Allman, a founder of the Allman Brothers, and is known for rock music, but maybe, if asked, he'll do a blues number or two.

CHANGES ARE SHAKING UP A SIMPLE LIFE

11.4.2007

The squirrels come up the stairs and eat out of Paul Manning's hand. He feeds them peanuts. Unsalted, of course. He can tell the squirrels apart. One is Rocky. Another is Coontail. His favorite was Mary. She would jump onto his lap. I asked how he knew that particular squirrel was a female. She was pregnant, he said.

During her pregnancy, she would eat peanuts until she was full, and then she would take one, run off and bury it, and return for another. She eventually became a mother. Manning never saw her offspring. He told me she came to the porch one day, and then later he heard her screeching and he was sure she was scolding her children, trying to get them to follow her to the porch, but they wouldn't do it. Then he didn't see Mary again.

After several days, his uncle, Dennis Larose, told him that Mary had been hit by a car. "I didn't want to tell you, but I guess you should know," Larose said.

I wrote about Manning and Larose two weeks ago. They shared an apartment near the intersection of Manchester and McCausland in southwest St. Louis. Manning, who is 49, was driving his uncle's 1989 Dodge truck one evening last month when he got pulled over for a traffic violation. Police found a small amount of marijuana and some pills in the truck. Manning was arrested and taken to jail.

The next morning, Larose fell and broke his hip. He was taken to a nursing home. He was 70 years old. He told me that any pills in his truck belonged to him. He took pills because of his lung cancer, he said. He had already stopped chemotherapy and radiation.

Bond was set for Manning at $10,000. He could not come up with that kind of money, so he stayed in jail for a couple of weeks. I visited him. He told me he was on disability because of a head injury. Or maybe it was for a back injury. He wasn't sure. He had hurt his back, and then later he hurt his head. He was not exactly sure how much he received each month. "I think I used to get $600, but now I get $400. I think I didn't do something," he told me.

I wrote a column about his situation, and some relatives called a bondsman and got him out. One of his sisters said they waited for Manning to call for a ride home.

"Paul never called anyone. He just took MetroLink and a bus and got back to the flat he shares with Uncle Denny. I went to see him after he got home, and he was an emotional wreck," his sister said.

He was released from jail on Oct. 24 and two days later, a friend took him to see his uncle. His uncle was in bad shape. Manning's friend had the presence of mind to write a statement in which the uncle said that the prescription medicine in the truck belonged to him, and not Manning. The signature is almost illegible, but the note is notarized.

Larose died the next day.

I stopped by to see Manning on Friday afternoon. A squirrel was drinking from a water dish on the front porch. It darted away when I approached.

Manning said jail was an ordeal. Three people in a two-man cell. "No room for pacing," he said. He is not a large man. About 5-foot-5 and 110 pounds. I asked if he had trouble with any of the inmates. No, he said. The majority of the people he met were good people, he said. He said he heard a lot of stories about people who didn't deserve to be in jail.

His future remains uncertain. He said he does not believe he can keep the apartment he shared with his uncle. He said the rent would be too high. He has two offers to move in with people, and although he values his independence, at least it doesn't seem like homelessness will be a problem.

His sister told me that the family would help him try to work out the disability situation, and Manning showed me a business card from licensed clinical social worker with the Department of Mental Health. He said he would call her. She might have been his caseworker, he said.

Manning went to the impound lot to get the truck, but the people there told him that because the title was not in his name, he would have to go through a legal process that seemed complicated. Plus, the storage fees already exceed the value of the vehicle. And what would he do for insurance?

His legal status is cloudy. There is still the matter of the marijuana. His sister said the bondsman suggested he hire a private attorney, but that seems beyond his means.

Still, he is out of jail – at least for now. But he misses his uncle. Mary, too. Before I left, he showed me her photograph.

MENTAL ILLNESS, FAMILY TIE COMPLICATE MURDER TRIAL

2.1.2009

Bailiff Vern Betts said in a stern voice, "Careful now. Prisoner coming through." Instinctively, the two women standing in the aisle of the courtroom moved aside to let Betts lead the prisoner past. Then Betts laughed, and the two women realized that the prisoner was, of course, their nephew, the man whom they'd come to support, and they laughed, too. The prisoner seemed a tad confused – although that could have been my imagination – and then he laughed, and he and his aunts embraced and kissed.

It was a brief, light moment in an otherwise heavy week.

The prisoner, Jamal Whitt, was on trial for the murders of Mary Morant and Rodney Staples.

Often at trials I have the sense that I am seeing a very small slice of a very big picture. It's like trying to make sense of a thick book by reading a couple of pages. This trial was very much like that.

Morant was Whitt's grandmother. She was 64. She was supposed to have been romantically involved with Staples. He was 39. Whitt had a large contingent of family at the trial. I asked several of them about the alleged romance between Morant and Staples. They rolled their eyes. They shrugged their shoulders. Did Morant have a lot of money? No, she did not. Everybody seemed to agree to that.

By the way, the murders occurred in April 2005. Whitt was arrested immediately. Why then was he just now going to trial?

There had been some question about his mental condition. He has been diagnosed with schizophrenia and an anti-social personality disorder. Before the murders, he had been admitted on four occasions to the Metropolitan St. Louis Psychiatric Center. Then there were the murders themselves. One of the cops told me the scene looked like something out of a horror movie. Knives and blood all over. Morant had been strangled, but the murder of Staples was gruesome. One of his lungs was visible. His body had been sexually mutilated. One could look at the photos of the crime scene and conclude that this was not the work of a person in his right mind.

But for purposes of legal culpability, the sanity bar is set low. You have to know right from wrong. As for being competent to stand trial, that bar is low, too. You have to be able to understand the charges against you and you have to be able to assist in your own defense.

Still, it was a while before the state concluded that Whitt was ready for trial. State psychologist Ericia Kempker testified that Whitt's schizophrenia is now in full remission. Actually, Whitt's mental condition was not officially at issue. The defense made no argument about his ability to stand trial. Kempker testified at the request of Judge Mark Neill. This defendant is competent to stand trial, she said. She also said that she believed he had been malingering at the Department of Corrections diagnostic center in Fulton. That is, feigning mental illness after he had been in remission.

A defendant has the right to a trial by jury, but Whitt, through his attorney, Annette Llewellyn, a veteran of the Public Defender's office, waived that right. So Llewelyn and assistant circuit attorney Rachel Smith pitched their cases directly to the judge.

Whitt lived with his grandmother. He has maintained from the beginning that he killed Staples only after he discovered Staples attacking his grandmother. So the defense was arguing that in the death of Staples, Whitt was guilty only of voluntary manslaughter, that the crime was provoked by sudden passion, and that he was not guilty of the murder of his grandmother.

The state bore the burden of proving beyond a reasonable doubt that he had murdered them both. How do you refute a person's story when he is the only survivor?

Emotions were high. Whitt's mother had a difficult time containing herself. Perhaps that is not surprising. After all, she believed that her son had, in effect, come to the defense of her mother. The state was alleging that he had killed her.

Emile Whitt, the father of the defendant, had to be admonished when he objected to a line of questioning, a line of questioning that seemed insignificant to me. A police officer was describing the scene in the lobby of the apartment building on the night of the murder.

During a break, I asked him about his outburst. He said he thought the prosecutor was nodding at the police officer, coaching him. I asked if his son had always had mental problems. Yes, he said. He belongs in a hospital, he said. He was always slow and other children picked on him, he said. How about education? He got as far as his freshman year at Sumner High School, the father said. He wanted to play football, he said.

Perhaps he could have played on the line. He is not tall, but he is heavy. He is now 24. The murders occurred shortly before he turned 21.

The key testimony, I thought, was delivered Thursday afternoon near the end of the trial. Dr. Kamal Sabharwal from the medical examiner's office said there was no scientific way to determine which victim had been killed first, but the bottom of Morant's socks were soaked in Staples' blood. His body had been found in the bedroom. Her body was in the hall between the bedroom and the kitchen, with her feet in the kitchen. There was little blood around her body, so it would seem the only way her socks could have become drenched in blood would be if she had stepped in some. That would indicate that Staples had been attacked first.

It seemed like something out of Sherlock Holmes.

The defense case consisted of two aunts testifying that Whitt had been close to his grandmother. He did not testify. He had long ago given his story to the police, and a tape of that statement was played at his trial. Still, the judge was required to ask him about his decision not to take the stand. You have been here all week and you have heard the evidence, the judge began. Whitt must have looked confused, because the judge spoke again. You were here Monday, right? And Tuesday, and Wednesday and today? Whitt nodded. I wondered if the psychologist would say he was malingering. Not that it matters. Being slow, or even confused, is not a legal defense.

The judge took the case under submission. He said he would announce his verdict Friday.

WHAT WOULD JURY SAY IN BEAUTY VS. A-B?

5.28.2010

Francine Katz is a very attractive woman. She is brainy, too. I knew she was intelligent even before I met her. She used to be vice president of communications for Anheuser-Busch, and she was the first woman to sit on the company's strategy committee. You don't reach those heights without some smarts.

The attractive part I didn't know about until Wednesday. She has filed a lawsuit against Anheuser-Busch alleging gender discrimination. There was a hearing on that lawsuit Wednesday. I wandered into the courtroom.

She was sitting in the front row with her family. She was dressed stylishly, but tastefully. Because I have written about her case, she recognized me and introduced herself.

When I wrote about her lawsuit in November, I wrote that she would not want me on her jury. "In fact, there are probably a lot of guys who ought not sit on this jury. That's because one of her complaints is that the brewery encouraged a 'frat party' atmosphere, to which many guys would respond, 'It's a brewery!'"

Perhaps that was a flippant comment, but after meeting Katz, I am more convinced than ever that she would not want me on her jury.

That's because I have long believed that attractive, smart women travel downstream. That is, the current is always with them. Attractive women are noticed. Smart, attractive women might say they are noticed for the wrong reasons, but still, they are noticed.

Katz was promoted out of the legal department and given the vice president of communications job when she was in her early 40s.

Was she the smartest person in the legal department? Maybe she was, but even so, there are a lot of very smart people in the corporate world who never get noticed.

So I have a difficult time thinking that attractive women are victims of discrimination.

Of course, technically, legally, they can be victims of discrimination. But in a broader sense, they're like athletes. They have a certain self-confidence that comes from living in a world in which they are generally admired, a world in which people are nice to them. Many of us don't live in that world.

After the hearing, I was in the hallway and saw a man waiting for an elevator. He was overweight. I thought, "He knows something about discrimination."

People seldom figure that fat guys are smart. Or that homely people are innocent. Maybe you saw the story in this paper Thursday about a national study showing that jurors are 22 percent more likely to convict an unattractive defendant than an attractive one – with the same set of facts. I read that and thought, "Only 22 percent more likely?"

Attractive people get breaks. We all know that. So what happens when an attractive person files a discrimination lawsuit and a homely person gets on the jury?

That would concern me if I were Katz. What if a female juror was not invited to prom and never got over it? She might look at an attractive woman like Katz, and think, "Discrimination? Are you kidding me? What do you know about waiting for the phone to ring?"

I should be clear that I am not talking about the merits of this particular case. For that matter, the hearing wasn't about the merits of the case. The hearing was about whether there should be a case.

Attorney Gerard Carmody, representing Anheuser-Busch, argued that all brewery employees, including officers, had agreed to submit all employment disputes to binding arbitration. Attorney Mary Anne Sedey, representing Katz, argued that the agreement to which Carmody referred was nullified when the brewery was sold. She also argued that arbitration does not allow the amount of discovery that is necessary in an employment discrimination case.

Frankly, I am rooting for Sedey.

It would be a fun case. According to earlier stories about the lawsuit, Katz replaced John Jacobs as vice president of communications and received, in her first year, less than half of what he received in his final year. Still, she received $500,000.

Sedey is a persuasive attorney, but how much sympathy will ordinary people have for somebody who made $500,000?

For that matter, filings in the case showed that the aggregate value of equities – whatever that is – for Katz when the brewery was sold was $12,216,182. How do you find a jury in this city that will believe somebody with that kind of pay-out was a victim of discrimination?

On the other hand, people are still angry at the brewery for being sold. So maybe they will want to punish the new owners.

Unless the jurors are homely. If they are, the odds swing toward the brewery.

A LIFETIME OF BRIGHTENING LIVES BROUGHT JOY INTO VOLUNTEER'S HEART

2.17.2008

Gwen was born 81 years ago on a farm near Stanford, Ill. She was the second child of Robert and Leota Kampf. Robert was killed in a car-train accident when Gwen was about 5 years old. Leota then married another farmer, Wallace Kaufman.

After finishing high school, Gwen went to Eureka College. While she was there, the school's most famous alum, Ronald Reagan, visited for a pumpkin festival. He was, at the time, an actor. That was the sort of glamorous world to which Gwen aspired. She wanted to be a fashion designer, or an artist. But while the Kaufman family farm supported the family, it did not do much more than that. There was not enough money to keep Gwen in school. She moved to Peoria to live with a cousin. She got a job in a drugstore.

John Kinslowe called on that drugstore as a salesman for Johnson and Johnson. This was shortly after World War II. Kinslowe had served in Europe. He was from the big city of St. Louis. Actually, his mother had grown up on a farm in what is now the Meacham Park section of Kirkwood.

John and Gwen dated and then married. Gwen designed and made her own wedding dress. They moved to St. Louis. They soon had four children. They bought a small house in Jefferson County with some kind of special veterans' assistance. They then sold that house and moved to Crestwood.

As a salesman, John was often on the road. The responsibility of raising the kids belonged to Gwen. She also watched the children of another family while their mother worked. When her kids and the other children grew up and left for college, Gwen started volunteering with the Girl Scouts. She was the crafts instructor at the Girl Scouts day camp for 20 years. She also volunteered at Head Start in Meacham Park.

But her real love was St. Joseph's Hospital in Kirkwood. She became a Pink Lady Volunteer in about 1970. She delivered mail to patients. She made carnations. Mostly, though, she was known for working at the front desk. People remembered her. She was a familiar and friendly face. She logged more than 28,000 hours of volunteer time at the hospital.

She was interviewed by Senior Circuit St. Louis in 1997. "When I pull in to my garage at night I always feel so much better than I did when I left that morning," she said. "I think back over the day and I think, well, you made somebody laugh, or someone made you laugh, or you shared a joke. Sometimes one of the older patients will see me and say, 'Hey, I knew you when I was in the hospital 15 years ago.' The thing is, when you brighten someone else's day, your day is fulfilled. I know that sounds kind of Pollyanna-ish, but it's true."

Her husband died in 1992. Her oldest child, Carol, died of cancer several years ago. Gwen became ill in November. She spent a few days in the hospital – St. Joseph's, of course – and then went to a nursing home to recuperate. She returned to her home in Crestwood on Christmas Eve. She wanted to get back to her volunteer work so she could make 30,000 hours.

But she became increasingly frail. Her son, David, took her back to the hospital a week ago Thursday. There was a problem with her colon. She needed surgery. She was weak, but seemed to be at peace. If it's my time, it's my time, she said.

While David and his sisters, Polly and Jan, were in the waiting room during their mother's surgery, news came of the shooting at the nearby Kirkwood City Hall. But there wasn't much time to dwell on it – the family was in the midst of its own drama. Gwen survived the surgery. On Friday morning, she seemed to be doing pretty well. Then she began going downhill. She died on Saturday.

The funeral notice appeared in small type in the newspaper the next day. By the way, despite a life of service, she had been in this newspaper on only two other occasions – both in the readers' recipe exchange column.

In 1994, she responded to a request for a pulled taffy recipe, and in 1996, she offered a recipe for Vienna Crescents. And then her funeral notice: "Kinslowe, Gwen, 81, passed suddenly, February 9, 2007. Gwen Kinslowe is survived by her loving children Polly, Jan and David, preceded in death by her daughter Carol. Gwen was put on this earth to help others all her life. She volunteered at Lindbergh schools, Head Start, Girl Scout troop 626 and over 28,000 hours at St. Joseph Hospital where she was a comfort to thousands and a friend to many: Visitation Tuesday, 4-7 p.m. ...'"

It so happens that there was also a visitation at Bopp Chapel on Tuesday night for Connie Karr, a member of the Kirkwood City Council and a victim of the shooting. Karr was a wonderful person and had a thousand friends. When my wife and I arrived at the chapel, there was a two-hour wait to see her family. If you were in that line and happened to glance over at the smaller room and wondered about the person being remembered in that room, well, now you know. Two good people were remembered at Bopp that night.

CHANGING TIMES: NOW NOT SPARING THE ROD LEADS TO A DAY IN COURT

9.2.2007

Deborah Vassas is a single mother. She lives with her 9-year-old son, Andrew, in a mobile home on Highway Y not far from the Missouri town of Foley. She is 45, trim and has long blond hair. She wore a blue dress to court on Tuesday. She was accused of assaulting her son.

She sat at the defense table and listened as Peter Lassiter, a Lincoln County assistant prosecutor, queried prospective jurors.

"Does everyone agree that parental discipline can go too far? If you agree with that, would you please raise your hand." A sea of hands went up. The prospective jurors filled the gallery on one side of the courtroom. The other side was mostly empty, except for a small group of the defendant's supporters. Andrew was among them. He was sitting with his grandmother. Her name is Sharon Holmes. She raised seven children. She did not think much of the case against her daughter.

"If this sort of thing had been going on when I was raising my kids, I'd be doing life without parole," she told me.

The state was alleging that on a February morning in 2006, Vassas pushed Andrew, who was then 7, with such force that he fell back, and his head knocked a hole in the wall. The defense was arguing that his head had merely dented the wall and his injuries were minimal. Furthermore, there was reason for Vassas to be angry. Andrew had been messing around that morning, playing video games, and had missed the school bus. He had done so willfully, knowing that his mother did not have a car and that if he missed the bus, he wouldn't have to go to school. He had missed the bus eight times in the previous two months.

If he had indeed intended to miss school, his plan did not work. Vassas hiked to her mother's house, borrowed her mother's car and drove Andrew to school.

When he got there, he complained to a teacher that his head hurt. Soon he was talking to the school counselor.

As the law requires, the counselor reported the incident to the Division of Family Services and the police. A social worker and a sheriff's deputy were dispatched to the mobile home. Vassas confessed. That is, she admitted shoving her son, and she said she was sorry she had lost her temper.

She was charged with third-degree assault. That is a misdemeanor. The state offered her a deal. If she agreed to plead guilty, she would be given one year of unsupervised probation.

Vassas said there was no way she would plead guilty to assaulting her son. "I am a great mother," is the way she explained it to me.

And so the case went to trial.

In a sense, it was a sociology study. There was a time in this country when physical discipline was widely accepted. Parents were warned that sparing the rod would spoil the child. But is physical discipline still acceptable? Also, there was a geographical component. Perhaps old-fashioned values have hung on in the rural areas. On the other hand, Lincoln County used to be more rural than it is now. Have times changed? Has Lincoln County changed?

In his opening statement, Lassiter said that Vassas had gone too far, and the jury should hold her responsible. Lincoln County public defender Tom Gabel represented Vassas. In his opening statement, he made the point that Andrew has not missed the bus in the 18 months since the incident.

Andrew testified. Technically, he was a witness for the state, but his testimony seemed to add little to the state's case. Yes, his mom had been angry at him. Yes, she had pushed him. No, he had not been seriously hurt.

The school counselor testified but did not seem hostile to Vassas. Perhaps the state's strongest witness was the social worker. Shoving a child into a wall with that kind of force is not appropriate discipline, she said. But she also testified that she had determined that it was a one-time incident and she had not removed the child from the home.

Vassas took the stand. She said she used to sell cars for a dealership and had been given a car to drive. When she was laid off, she had no transportation. Her son knew that. "He knows I'm a pushover so he'd miss the bus so he could stay home and hang out," she said. So yes, she had lost her temper because she felt he had intentionally missed the bus again.

In his closing statement, Lassiter argued that Vassas' idea of discipline had crossed over into abuse. Gabel dismissed that notion. Abuse is when you don't correct the child because then in a few years he'll be sitting in that chair, Gabel said, pointing to a chair at the defense table.

While we waited for the jury to return with a verdict, I chatted with Vassas. She said the only time she had ever spanked Andrew was when he had wandered into the woods when he was 3.

After deliberating for less than an hour, the jury returned with a not guilty verdict. Nobody seemed happier than Andrew.

Bill McClellan • Gently Down the Stream

INVESTIGATOR HAS HIS EYE OUT FOR CHEATERS

2.3.2010

Brian Randant and I walked into a bar in St. Charles early one evening last week. Several young women were at one end of the bar. They were laughing and talking with one another. Maybe they worked together and were enjoying a happy hour before going home.

At the other end of the bar were a group of guys. They were in blue-collar work clothes. They seemed to know the bartender well. Regulars at the bar, I'd guess.

Randant and I gave the two groups a brief glance and then moved to a table.

"There they are," he said, but he didn't point. "The couple playing pool."

There were several pool tables across the room. I stole a quick look at the couple, and when I realized they were lost in their own world, I allowed myself a longer look.

She was blond, pretty and small. I knew she was 40, but she looked younger. Her billiards partner was thin and had long, dark hair. He was younger than the woman by a few years.

Randant already had shown me her photo. It was a heart-breaking picture. She was smiling in front of a Christmas tree. The heart-breaking thing was that her husband had given the photo to Randant, a private investigator. His company is called Catch Em' Cheatin.' If you hire him, he will follow your spouse around. If he finds evidence, he will take videos indicating that your spouse is cheating.

I say "indicating" because he does not try to sneak up to windows and take videos of people inside apartments or motel rooms. Instead, he'll take videos of people coming out of apartments or motels. Or videos of people hugging or sneaking a quick kiss in a parking lot.

He wasn't taking pictures in the bar. He was just giving me an idea of the business.

After the husband hired him – at $75 an hour for a minimum of four hours – Randant had plotted his strategy. This was supposed to be the woman's night out with the girls. So Randant had two of his employees follow her. They followed her to the bar. There was a guy waiting for her.

Randant and I were at a restaurant near the woman's home. The employee called to tell us where she was. We drove to the bar.

We chatted at the table while they played pool. I asked what would happen next. He said that when the couple left, his employees would follow them. If they went to an apartment or motel, they'd get videos of them when they left the apartment or motel. That's considered pretty good proof in this business.

I asked Randant if his business was hurt at all by the recession. Just the opposite, he said. When the economy goes bad, his business gets better. He has a theory about that. He figures that relationships get frayed when people have money problems. Or maybe when reality gets bad, people try to escape it.

Actually, he has theories about a lot of things related to cheating. He thinks a lot of guys cheat for the excitement of cheating. He thinks most women are less likely to cheat on a whim. For them, it's a more serious thing.

It gets complicated, he said. And seamy. He said he'd rather own a restaurant. But he added that his job is not to figure out why people cheat, only to catch them doing it.

He said that Fridays and Mondays are big nights for cheating. That's because most people use work as an excuse for staying out late. If the weekends are out, Friday becomes emotional because the cheater won't see his or her lover until Monday, and Mondays are big because the cheater hasn't seen his or her lover for two days.

Are there many false alarms in this business? Randant said a man will hire him if he suspects his wife is cheating, and quite often that suspicion will prove unfounded. But by the time a woman hires him, she pretty much knows, he said.

By the way, sometimes a man will be angry that Randant has found no indication that his wife is cheating. Maybe it's because he's cheating, Randant said. Again, it's complicated.

Any cases he won't take? If a guy tells Randant that he's going to beat the hell out of his wife if she's cheating, Randant won't take the case. Also, no police officers. "If either of these two were cops, we wouldn't be here," he said about the couple playing pool.

Shortly thereafter, our quarry and her friend left. Randant and I stayed behind. A few minutes later, he got a phone call. The couple had gone to another bar.

"We can't go," he said. "They might recognize us."

The next day, Randant called. After the couple left that second bar, they went to a third bar, and then they went their separate ways. No motel, no apartment.

Well, who knows? There's nothing wrong with playing pool with a friend. That's what I thought – hoped, actually, as I recalled the photograph – until Randant said they had video of them kissing and hugging in the parking lot after they left that third bar.

Bill McClellan • Gently Down the Stream

ST. LOUIS IS TRULY SOMETHING SPECIAL

7.8.2009

There is something magical about living in St. Louis and going to the Muny in Forest Park to see "Meet Me in St. Louis."

Maybe if I lived in Tulsa, I'd be a big fan of "Oklahoma," but I don't think so. "Oklahoma" is a wonderful musical, but it doesn't speak to the people of Oklahoma today. It's about a time that is long gone.

That is not the case with "Meet Me in St. Louis." That play speaks to the people of St. Louis. It shouts to us. I'm thinking of one line in particular, and I'll get to that line in a minute, but first I want to say that I do not intend to encroach upon the territory of my friend and colleague Judy Newmark, whose review of this production appears on Page A15. This column is not intended as a review, and I will not be saying that this actor did well, and this actor did not, although I will have to say that two actors were miscast, but that, too, I will put aside for a moment.

I trust there is no need to review the plot. The Smiths live in St. Louis in the days before the World's Fair of 1904. Mr. Smith is offered a promotion that would take him to New York. He tells the family, and they get upset. They don't want to leave St. Louis.

That cuts to the quick, doesn't it? You know our history. Back when the country was founded, the successful people had no reason to leave the East Coast. The less successful pushed west. This clump of unsuccessful people reached St. Louis. The adventurous ones pushed on. The slackers stayed here. Much later, we built the Gateway Arch to honor the people who had the gumption to keep going. We are the only city in the world that has a memorial to honor those who left.

So this whole thing about leaving and not leaving is in our DNA.

Although our city's founders were slackers, they did do a couple of things right.

Foremost among these things is the Muny. It is the largest outdoor theater in the country. It is a wonderful venue, and every few years, it presents "Meet Me in St. Louis."

I am not one to tell people what to do, but there are two things that every St. Louisan ought to do – catch Chuck Berry at his monthly show at Blueberry Hill in the Delmar Loop, and see a production of "Meet Me in St. Louis" at the Muny.

This year's production opened Monday and will run through Saturday.

I've seen it before, so I know how it turns out, but still, when the father relented and decided not to take the promotion, I almost cried for joy. And then he shouted the line that spoke to us all. "We'll stay here until we all rot!" he shouted.

"Amen! Amen!" is the way people in church might have responded, but theatergoers are a more refined crowd, and we merely murmured our approval. "Yes, we will stay here until we all rot," we whispered to each other. Haven't we all made that decision? Isn't it good to see it validated on stage?

I mentioned that two actors were miscast. One was Stephen Bogardus, who played the father and shouted the line that electrified us all. He did a nice job as the father, but I saw him after the show, and he was much too young to be the father. The father should be somebody about my age. Aren't there any mature actors available? Then I caught a glimpse of Lewis Stadlen, who played the grandfather. No way should he be younger than me!

Admittedly, I have reached the age where if I go out to hear a band, I seldom know a member of the band, but I often know the parents of a member of the band.

So it was with this production.

One of the members of the ensemble was Jordan Newmark. Her mother is my aforementioned colleague. I don't mean to embarrass Jordan, but let me quote from a story her mother wrote years ago about the morning after Jordan's birth when the pediatrician came into the room. "'So,' I asked. 'Is she perfect?' 'Well,' said the pediatrician. Imagine a huge black pit. Imagine hurtling down it, with nothing to break your fall and no bottom in sight."

There was a problem with Jordan's heart. Dr. Tony Hernandez, a pediatric cardiologist, successfully performed the delicate operation to repair the heart. Several years later, Jordan was the St. Louis Heart Association's Heart Child, and her mother wrote the story quoted above. By that time, Hernandez was dead. He died of a heart attack. He was 58.

Jordan went on to the University of Michigan and has begun a career in theater.

I thought about that, and then of course I thought about my own kids, and how good life has been for us in St. Louis, and as I do every time I see this play, I started to cry.

"Meet Me in St. Louis" at the Muny. It's something special.

DAD'S INVESTMENT WAS PIE IN THE SKY

4.30.2010

Art McClellan never owned a certificate of deposit or a bond or a share of stock, but he bought a house when he returned to Chicago after the war, and my sister and I were raised in that house.

While we were still little, my father bought a piece of property in Michigan and he built a little cottage on that property, and my mother, grandmother and sister and I spent our summers in that cottage.

I was not alive when my father bought the house in Chicago, but I'm sure he inspected that house closely. I was a child when he bought the property in Michigan, but there are certain things I can recall.

He bought it from a weathered old Dutchman, Mr. Van Blois. I do not know his first name. He was known as Van, and I believe he owned a lot of property.

Van drove an old car. He wore old clothes. So my father, who drove an old car and wore old clothes, liked him. We drove to Michigan to visit with Van several times before my father bought the property.

Both of those purchases turned out well.

Years later, my dad bought a piece of property in Colorado. At the time, I was living in Arizona and my sister was in New Mexico, so it probably made sense to my dad to buy a piece of property in the West. He did not look at the property before he bought it. He saw an ad in a magazine about a model city that was going to be built at the foot of the Rockies. He bought a lot for $3,500. He paid cash.

A couple of years after his purchase, I drove to Colorado to look at his property. The city had not yet been constructed. There were no homes, no paved roads. It was very hilly terrain. My father's small plot was on the side of a steep hill.

There was a salesman in a dingy office in a shed, and I told him the whole thing seemed like a scam. You couldn't build a house on my father's property, I said. It's too steep. You use stilts, the salesman said.

There was no sense getting angry with him. He was just an employee, more of a caretaker than a salesman. Nobody who stopped by would ever buy. I'm sure the fellow would have rather been working at a legitimate development. The guys responsible for this scam – guys who didn't drive old cars and wear old clothes – were off-site.

I never mentioned to my father that I had visited his property.

My sister died, my mother died, and then my father died. I inherited the property.

Every year I got a tax bill in the mail. My bill was $34.20.

Every year I paid it. I can't explain why. Maybe part of it had to do with the hope that a Paul McKee of the Rockies would someday come forward with a transformational plan for the area, and maybe my lot would be the last remaining piece of the puzzle.

Or maybe it had to do with sentimentality. This scrubby little hillside lot represented a dream to my father. It was an investment, the only pure investment he had ever made. After all, the house in Chicago was our home, and the cottage in Michigan was a summer place.

Occasionally, I'd get mailings about my property. I remember one from World Wide Investments. "Sell your Colorado property for top dollar!"

I called the company to ask what "top dollar" meant. Maybe around $30,000, a woman said. I was flabbergasted. Have you seen my property? I asked. It's on the side of a steep hill. I asked if there was gold, or oil, under my hill.

She laughed and said that World Wide was recruiting foreign investors. Maybe somebody from Japan would buy my lot.

I had to think about that. Did I really want to be part of a scam? I thought for only a second. After all, my dad had been on Guadalcanal. He'd get a kick out of me scamming the Japanese. I'm in, I said.

Then the woman explained that I would have to pay several hundred dollars for marketing fees to try to facilitate a sale. I thought of the saying: If you sit down at the game and don't know who the sucker is, it's you. I declined the offer.

Years passed.

I got a letter last week from Reliant Land Trust in Oregon. The company was buying land in Colorado. I called the number and said that I was interested in selling. The woman told me I would receive a firm offer within a week.

It came Thursday.

The offer is $247.

That's probably fair, but it's hard to put a price tag on a dream.

MOTIVE FOR MURDER MAY NEVER BE KNOWN

10.12.2008

The state is not required to prove motive in a murder case, and that is a good thing, because the motive is often so totally inconsequential – a cross word, a disrespectful glance – that a juror with middle-class sensibilities might well reject the notion that so much could be lost over so little.

I thought about that as I sat through last week's speed-dial case against LaShawn Jordan. He was charged with first-degree murder in connection with the shooting death of Louis Davis in November 2006.

I say speed-dial because the case zipped along so quickly. Prosecutor Dwight Warren began presenting his case Tuesday afternoon. Six people, including three eyewitnesses, testified for the state. Their combined testimony – and the resultant cross-examinations – took about one hour. Jordan was the only witness presented by his attorney, Lyn Ruess. Jordan's testimony was brief. Except for closing arguments, that was it.

According to the state's witnesses, Davis, 35, and Jordan, 16, were standing in a gangway next to a house in the 5000 block of Arlington. It was late afternoon. They had a conversation. Perhaps voices were raised. Davis left and, as he walked away, Jordan shot him three times in the back. Jordan walked over to the body. He may have tried to fire again, and if so, the gun jammed. He banged the gun against his leg.

He was later arrested. From jail, he wrote several letters to a young female friend. He asked her to urge a friend – who was one of the eyewitnesses – to change his story. "Just look at it like your carry a major part of the 50ty on yo back, and by all means represent the true meaning of fidelity and loyalty," he wrote. He signed the letter with his street name, Static. The return address on that letter was Mr. Untouchable, 5300 Moneytalk, St. Louis, MO.

By the way, the teenager who received the letters did not testify. Instead, another woman verified that the handwriting in the letters was that of Jordan.

This woman was Cheryl Davis, the victim's sister. She said that her family and Jordan's family were friends, and Jordan had stayed with her in the past.

The state's case made no mention of motive. "We have no position on that," Warren told me.

In his testimony, though, Jordan discussed motive. Ruess asked him whether he knew the three young men who had told the jury that he shot Louis Davis. Yes, they're my co-workers, he said. Co-workers? We sell drugs, he said. Crack cocaine. He said they were members of a gang, the 50 Street Crips. Tell us what happened regarding the shooting, Ruess said. "When did the drama start? Six months before the shooting," Jordan said.

The drama. I've heard narcotics detectives refer to the location of a drug sale as "the set." Life as a movie. Both sides share the lingo.

Jordan said they sold drugs in pairs. One carried the money, the other the drugs. Six months earlier, his partner had lost his pack of drugs. That's what Louis Davis had come to talk about, he said. Davis had pulled out a pistol and slapped him with it, Jordan said. Then he dropped the pistol, and Jordan picked it up and shot him with it, he said.

So the victim was some kind of drug kingpin?

As Jordan testified, a young man with dreadlocks stood up. He was with the victim's family and friends. He glared at Jordan and then stormed out of the courtroom. He had to pass me to do so. "Excuse me, sir," he said softly.

The next day, the jury convicted Jordan of second-degree murder and armed criminal action. The jury recommended a sentence of 30 years for the murder and 20 years for the armed criminal action.

As for Jordan's story, I was dubious. I checked with the Department of Corrections. Louis Davis had never been in prison. He had been on probation once for a weapons charge. It seemed unlikely that he had been a drug dealer and had escaped detection for so long.

Friday morning, I drove to the scene of the shooting in the 5000 block of Arlington. I wondered if things were any quieter. After all, Jordan was gone, and one of his "co-workers" had testified that he was now living in Kansas City. Another "co-worker" had the look of a fellow in custody, although that's a guess since he's a juvenile, and his record is closed. Still, it seemed like the old gang might be breaking up.

I saw a man and a woman sitting on a porch. "Quieter?" said the woman. She laughed. The man pointed to a makeshift memorial – stuffed toys and such – just down the street. It was a memorial to Stephano Wallace. He was 16 when he was shot and killed on the block in August. We talked a bit and I asked if I could use their names. "Oh, no!" the man said.

David Tillman was sitting on a nearby porch. He is Louis Davis' stepfather. I had just introduced myself when Cheryl Davis, who had testified about Jordan's handwriting, came out of the house. I asked about Jordan's assertion that her brother was some kind of drug dealer. She laughed. She said that Davis sometimes stayed with his girlfriend's mother, and he sometimes stayed with a sister. He was basically homeless, she said.

And the young man with dreadlocks who was so polite?

That's his son, Louis Jr., and he was upset that Jordan was claiming that Davis was a drug dealer, she said.

If he wasn't a drug dealer, then what was the motive? She shrugged. I looked to Tillman. He shrugged, too.

Bill McClellan • Gently Down the Stream

THE VERY RICH NEED TO HEAR THAT THEY'LL BE SEEN AS CHINTZY

4.14.2008

F. Scott Fitzgerald wrote, "Let me tell you about the very rich. They are different from you and me."

He was right. The very rich have problems that the rest of us don't have. I thought about that when I read a story in the most recent St. Louis Business Journal. The story was written by Christopher Tritto, and it was about a group of former Post-Dispatch employees who are starting an online newspaper called the St. Louis Beacon.

First of all, let me wish them well. Not only are they former colleagues, they are friends. Besides, the more the merrier. Competition is good.

But let's get back to the problems of the very rich. The story began this way: "Less than three years after selling the St. Louis Post-Dispatch to Lee Enterprises, Emily Rauh Pulitzer is helping a group of former Post-Dispatch reporters and editors launch an online news site designed to take aim at stories they say the daily newspaper fails to cover."

Her help is in the form of something called a challenge grant. The story said she has promised to give this new venture $500,000 over the next two years if it can raise another $1.5 million from other donors. That would be a total of $2 million, which is, according to the story, the amount my friends think they need to get established.

As you might imagine, I read this story with keen interest. You might think I said to myself, Emily Rauh Pulitzer is awfully generous. I did not. Just the opposite. She's being chintzy, is what I thought.

That's because the story also noted that she was Pulitzer Inc.'s largest individual shareholder and collected more than $414.5 million when Pulitzer Inc. sold itself to Lee Enterprises in 2005.

She was, of course, very rich even before the sale. She came from money herself, and then in 1973, she married Joseph Pulitzer III (who called himself Joseph Pulitzer Jr.)

He was extremely wealthy. By the way, he was 60. She was 39. So they had houses and money and art – oh, the art! – and when he died in 1993, most of the fortune was in a trust and so details were not made public, a fact the Business Journal noted at the time seemed odd considering the fortune had been "made from the sweat of prying reporters."

But one can assume that Emily Rauh Pulitzer did fine. I mention this just to note that she was very rich even before collecting $414.5 million in 2005.

So I thought to myself, If she wants to help these people with their new venture – and these are people who worked years and years for her late husband and whose efforts helped build his fortune – why not give them the $2 million they need? What does $1.5 million mean when you have at least $414 million. Would your standard of living suffer if you only had $412.5 million? Of course not. And another thing – why tie the gift up in some kind of challenge? Just give it.

So that's one problem that the very rich have. Even when they think they're being generous, people like me are going to think they're chintzy.

Which brings us to the second problem that the very rich have.

Nobody brings this sort of thing to their attention. If you or I do something people think is chintzy, people tell us. But the very rich? People are too busy currying favor. That might be especially true with Emily Rauh Pulitzer.

She controls a vast fortune, and she has no children.

Yikes. Every nonprofit in the country wants to be on her good side. That's not to mention the local nonprofit community, which is, I suspect, gripped by the fear that she might be inclined to be generous on a bigger stage. New York, perhaps.

Also, it would be naive to think that ordinary folks she encounters don't harbor secret dreams. I remember reading that her husband left $25,000 to his ski instructor in Switzerland.

So say you have some minor part in her life. You might think about that ski instructor. If so, would you be inclined to be critical? Would you say, "Only $500,000 to the online newspaper? These people originally were going to call their venture 'The Platform.' That was going to be in honor of your late husband and his legacy and the whole Pulitzer tradition. Why don't you just spring for another $1.5 million?"

Nobody says things like that to the very rich. Except me. And I'm saying it not to be spiteful or nasty, but to be helpful. It's the sort of thing a caring ski instructor might do.

LIKE AROMAS FROM A BAKERY, MEMORIES OF A GOOD LIFE LINGER

11.16.2007

When Pasquale "Lino" Gambaro was a high school student many years ago, he wanted to study Spanish and become an interpreter. That might seem like a strange ambition for a child of Italian immigrants, but sometimes an idea just gets hold of a person. Lino's father died before Lino could finish high school and he had to go to work in the family bakery, but still, he studied Spanish in his spare time. He would be back by the ovens, sitting in a chair, looking up words in the dictionary.

His nephew, Chris Gambaro, told me that story when I stopped by the Missouri Baking Company on Thursday morning to order pies and rolls for Thanksgiving.

This will be the first holiday season without Lino. He died in August. He was 91. He started working full time at the bakery when he had to drop out of high school and he never retired. He came to work every day, including the day he died.

On his final day, he came in an hour early at 4 a.m. He parked next to the bakery. That was strange. He always parked down the street a bit so customers could have the closer spots. But on that last day, he parked next to the bakery.

He came in and made it a point to speak to each of the night bakers. He spoke to his nephew. Then he started his daily tasks. He put the icing on the coconut drops. He carried some trays out to the front. Chris knew that the next task was making the pizza shells so he got the dough out, but Lino waved him off. I'm going home, he said. But he didn't. He sat down in the back of the bakery. Chris came over and asked him if he was all right. Yes, I'm fine, he said.

Maybe he was enjoying the smell of the place for the last time.

When my children were little, Lino used to take them into the back and get them cookies right out of the oven. To a person unaccustomed to the odors of a bakery, it was almost intoxicating.

Lino was more at home back by the ovens than out front, but it was out front that I first met him. I had come in for pizza dough. Lino was working at the counter and gave me a couple of lumps of dough. Am I supposed to let this rise? I asked. Yes, he said. How long? Do you drink? Lino asked. Yes, I said. Let it rise for about two beers, Lino said.

Lino never married. He lived a couple of blocks from the bakery with his sister, JoAnn. She married late in life, and Lino continued living with her and her husband, Derio. Derio did bookkeeping for the bakery. He died several years ago.

The Missouri Baking Company has always been a family business. It still is. JoAnn comes in almost every day. She is 90. In addition to Lino and JoAnn, there were four other brothers. Frank was a night baker. Steve was a cake man. Both are gone. Ben specialized in cookies and pastries. He still comes in almost every day. The fourth brother, John, was not a baker.

Chris and his sister, Mimi Lordo, are Ben's kids. They work at the bakery.

Mimi said that Lino tried to enlist during World War II but was turned down because of problems with his feet. So he just stayed at the bakery, stayed on the Hill. Without trying, he became a symbol of the neighborhood.

His funeral was held at St. Ambrose. The church was packed.

"Even now, some customers come in, realize he's gone, and they cry," Mimi said.

The bakery has retired Lino's oven mitts. Actually, Monsignor Sal Polizzi mounted them on a plaque. Under the mitts is a note written by the monsignor, but in Lino's spirit, in which Lino thanks God for everything, especially his family, and also for "granting me my last wish on this earth, that I should be called home to you my loving God while at the bakery."

Which is what happened. After sitting by the ovens for a while, he went out to his car. About 10 minutes later, one of the bakers noticed that he was still in the car. Chris went out to see if he was all right. He was gone.

By the way, one of the night bakers is originally from Mexico, and Lino used to speak to him in Spanish. While baking, of course, while baking.

Bill McClellan • Gently Down the Stream

JUDGE DECLINES TO SWALLOW STORY OF MAN WHO SOLD OTHER'S GOODS

3.25.2007

On a Saturday in late November, 74-year-old Larry Bode, a resident of Cape Girardeau, had a yard sale. The sale was informal to the point of being disorganized. Bode simply put boxes of things in the backyard. People pawed through the boxes and then bickered about the prices.

An antiques dealer, who makes a habit of visiting garage sales, made a couple of small purchases, and then went in the house. Amidst some junk, he saw some nice things. So he made Bode an offer – $2,000 for everything. Bode accepted.

But there was a problem: Bode didn't own the house. He didn't own any of the contents. He simply broke into the house and started hauling the contents into the backyard for a yard sale.

When the police contacted Bode – he had given the antiques dealer a bill of sale and had signed it – Bode admitted that he had not acquired the property in the conventional manner. That is, he had not bought it. He claimed ownership through "adverse possession." That's a common-law term that is roughly equivalent to "squatters' rights." In this case, nobody was living in the house, so Bode said he figured it had been abandoned. So he claimed it.

Actually, there is an adverse possession statute in Missouri. It says that if a person has been in possession of a piece of real estate for 30 years, he may bring an action to get title to the real estate, as long as the original owner has not been paying taxes on it during that 30 years. That is a far cry from "claiming" property that you think has been abandoned. So Bode was charged with two felonies – burglary and stealing.

The case went to trial Friday, and here was the defense: Burglary and stealing require the element of intent. If Bode sincerely believed that he was legally claiming the property – even if he was wrong in that belief – then he did not have the intent to commit a crime.

Assistant Public Defender Jennifer Booth represented Bode. She opted for a bench trial – that is, no jury, just a judge. Her theory was that a jury would dismiss this notion of "necessary intent" as legal mumble-jumble. I think she was right. During a break in the trial Friday morning, a man sitting in front of me turned to his friend and said, "If this works, I'm cleaning out your place tomorrow night."

There is another element to this case. It's one that a jury would not have been allowed to know unless the defendant were to testify – he did not – and the judge knew but was not supposed to consider. Bode has a criminal history. It's mostly for stealing and fraud.

In 1979, he was arrested for mail fraud, a federal offense. He was accused of submitting fraudulent credit card applications, using 56 names and 16 addresses. Even after he was arrested, he kept going, and managed to ring up $16,732 in fraudulent charges between his arrest and his trial. He was sentenced to three years.

He was eventually released to a halfway house in St. Louis, and while there, he prepared a number of phony tax returns and applied for $34,278 worth of refunds. He was sent back to prison.

When he got out, he found some billboards on the highway that said, "Rent Me." He painted his phone number on the billboards and tried to rent out the space.

That kind of history makes a person wonder about the contention that he did not have the intent to steal. The intent seems to have been there in the past.

Prosecutor Morley Swingle presented several witnesses. One was a neighbor who had bought some items at the yard sale. She said Bode had told her he had acquired the house for back taxes. Another neighbor said Bode had told her the same story. The antiques dealer said Bode had told him he had acquired the house after the owners died.

All of that hurt Bode, I thought. If he really believed in this adverse possession thing, why did he make up these other stories?

The final witness for the state was the elderly man who owned the house. He said he used it for storage.

The only witness the defense called was the detective who had questioned Bode. He said Bode had told him he had acquired the property through adverse possession.

Closing arguments were brief. Booth said there was reasonable doubt about intent. Swingle said there was nothing reasonable about breaking into somebody's house and selling his property.

Judge Benjamin F. Lewis sided with Swingle. If we were to validate this defense, nobody would be safe to go on vacation, the judge said. He then pronounced Bode guilty of burglary and stealing.

Sentencing will be Monday. Each of the charges carries a maximum of seven years.

Bill McClellan • Gently Down the Stream

IS CIVILIZATION IN DECLINE? YOU BET; LOOK AT RACETRACKS

6.10.2007

If you need more evidence of the decline of civilization, let me direct your gaze to the Illinois Legislature in Springfield. No, not the legislators themselves. They have not changed much over the years. Even when civilization was thriving – before the Beatles broke up, before free agency and expanded playoffs changed baseball, before "American Idol" and "Survivor" replaced quality programs like "Gunsmoke" and "Have Gun Will Travel" – Illinois legislators were of questionable character. No, the real sign of the decline of civilization can be seen in the latest effort to forge a comprehensive gaming bill.

Just the fact that there is something called a comprehensive gaming bill should concern us.

Government didn't used to have anything to do with gaming. Old-timers will remember something called the "numbers game." Young people know it as the lottery. Yes, the state moved in on the mob. Citizens were better served by the mob.

In 2005, the Illinois Gaming Board ruled that Penn National Gaming, a Pennsylvania company, would have to sell two of its three casinos, including the Argosy Casino at Alton, because, the board said, it was improper for one entity to own three of the state's nine casinos. A week and a half ago, Illinois Senate leaders decided to overrule the board. If that seems curious, consider that Penn National has given $500,000 to Illinois politicians in the past three years.

But again, there is nothing new about the rapacious nature of Illinois legislators.

What really disturbs me about the comprehensive gaming bill is this: The state's racetracks want slot machines.

That's because casinos have hurt racetracks. Apparently, there is only so much gambling money, and the more that goes to casinos, the less that goes to racetracks.

This is true all over the country. Racetracks have been struggling. Eighteen states have tried to revive the racing industry with slot machines.

This may or may not happen in Illinois. There are a number of other plans still under consideration, all of which would, in effect, transfer money from the casinos to the racetracks.

But what does it say about us as a society that slot machines could help racetracks?

Slot machines are for zombies. There is no thinking involved, no skill. In essence, you're playing against a computer that is programmed to pay out a certain percentage of what it takes in, and needless to say, that percentage is not 100.

Betting on the horses is entirely different. Thinking is involved. A person can study the racing form and try to figure things out. Of course, things don't always work out to form, but still, there is at least the illusion that there is such a thing as Smart Money. Also, such a thing as Dumb Money.

That is what I represent. I pay close attention to the horses' names. I try to determine if there is some connection between a horse's name and my life. For instance, last Tuesday I was at the track, and a horse named Hippie Sue was running. My friends were studying the forms, and talking about jockeys, and which horses were moving up or down in class, and so on and so forth, while I was daydreaming about a Sue I once knew. She got married on a garbage dump. Hippies used to do things like that. So I put $2 on Hippie Sue to win.

I would have been better off putting that money into a slot machine.

On the other hand, Mahie Dolly struck a certain memory in the sixth race, and I put $2 on her to win. She came charging toward the finish line neck and neck with Highlandtigerstar. Indeed, it was a photo finish. I lost, but my son had $2 on Highlandtigerstar.

By the way, I can't imagine a man taking his son to spend an afternoon playing the slots. What kind of father would do that? But an afternoon at the track? That's quality time.

So I hope the Illinois Legislature can do something to help the racing industry. I'd prefer that help to be something other than slot machines, but then again, I'm a nostalgic sort. I remember when civilization was going strong. In those days, Paris was a city, Hilton was a hotel chain, hippies got married on garbage dumps, and nobody had ever heard of a boat in a moat.

EVEN LAWYERS STUNG BY 'EVOLVING' ECONOMY

10.28.2009

The Chicago Bridge and Iron Co. was just a few blocks from my childhood home. It was a big place, a mysterious place, a place of noise and heat and fire. My mother worked there as a secretary. One day she walked into the office and another secretary said something like, "There is a big brown dog in the parking lot."

Although there were undoubtedly many big brown dogs roaming around at any given moment on the south side of Chicago, my mother had a sixth sense. She immediately went to the parking lot and looked around and sure enough, it was our dog. She took the dog home and went back to work.

I doubt that could happen today. For one thing, the factory near my home shut down long ago. The company still exists, but the corporate headquarters are now in the Netherlands. Perhaps there is a tax advantage to that. On the other hand, the Dutch have universal health care, which many people equate with socialism, and I have never suspected socialists of being light on corporate taxes.

At any rate, the key point is that the factory is gone.

So are secretaries.

Oh, there are a few left. But mostly, there are office managers and executive assistants, and they are related to secretaries the way birds are related to dinosaurs. They have evolved. And guess what? During the evolutionary process, the numbers dwindled. There are far fewer office managers and executive assistants than there were secretaries.

Of course, I have no evidence of this. It's all anecdotal.

My evidence is also anecdotal when I say that young people can't find work today. I have seen no statistics, but I am convinced that it's true. Among people my age – that is, people who have children entering the work force – it is the No. 1 topic of conversation.

What are young people supposed to do?

For years, we've known the economy was changing. The factories were closing. Secretaries and switchboard operators were becoming extinct. "What you need today is an education." That was the message we repeated endlessly.

Not that we had to convince them. I often looked at my kids and their friends, and thought, "How accomplished they are."

That was not just me being a goofy father. I remember talking with Jim Talent when he was in the U.S. Senate. He told me about the résumés he was getting from young people who wanted to work in his office. You wouldn't believe the things some of these kids have done, he said. They've written operas, or they've started companies, and they must have been doing it in their spare time because they're still in school. And they're getting straight A's!

Admittedly, my generation didn't set particularly high standards. I remember visiting the journalism department at Arizona State University several years after I had left the place without quite getting a degree. One of the professors saw me. He told me the department had improved. "No offense, Bill, but we wouldn't take somebody like you now."

I didn't take offense. I knew I wasn't a good student. Still, I got a job. That was a good thing about those days. You didn't have to set the world on fire to get a job.

Today even good students are having a difficult time getting jobs. Even good students from good schools are having trouble.

My daughter teaches high school biology in California. Two of her friends are engaged to young men who graduated last May from the law school at the University of California at Berkeley. Both young men had job offers at big firms, and then, shortly before graduation, the offers were rescinded. Delayed for a year, actually, and the young men were offered a portion of their salaries while they waited.

"That's a great deal," I said to my daughter. "You don't understand, Dad," she said. "They've got big law school loans to pay."

I mentioned this recently to a lawyer friend. Nobody's hiring, he said. People can't afford legal work right now. Life is going on, he said. Marriages are still crumbling, people are still getting arrested, but most people can't afford lawyers. Consequently, young people are graduating from law school and are unable to find jobs.

It's bad enough that the factories are closed, bad enough that the secretarial pools have gone dry. But that has been happening for some time now. This other thing is newer – unemployed college graduates, unemployed law school graduates. It's as if some unspoken intergenerational contract has been broken.

EVEN AT THE END, ORTHWEIN KEPT HIS OLD MONEY VALUES

8.18.2008

Not long ago, a tipster called this newspaper to report that James Orthwein was gravely ill. The person who answered the phone responded, who's James Orthwein?

Orthwein, who died Friday, would have been pleased.

In 1990, when his money was central to this city's efforts to land an expansion football team, a sportswriter asked Orthwein about his relative anonymity. How come more people hadn't heard of a guy who had enough money to buy an NFL team?

"I don't know of anybody that a lot of publicity has helped in this world," said Orthwein.

That is the quintessential attitude of Old Money. Class reveals itself by not revealing itself. It is always best to be understated and dignified. The clue to a person's identity is his middle name. So it was with James Busch Orthwein. His mother was the granddaughter of Adolphus Busch, one of the founders of Anheuser-Busch.

Although Orthwein didn't become "famous" until he got involved in football, he didn't just stay home and clip coupons. His father had founded the D'Arcy advertising agency, and Orthwein worked for it and eventually took it over. The business grew under his leadership.

Still, it was the football follies that made Orthwein a household name. His ill-fated partnership with Jerry Clinton was a story that defines our region.

You might remember those days. We had chased Bill Bidwill and his football team out of town. Most of us were fine without the NFL. In fact, we felt darned good about ourselves. Then-Mayor Vince Schoemehl, who was definitely not

Old Money and held understatement and dignity in the same low regard in which he held grammar, said this about NFL owners: "These are not reputable people, and I don't think it's becoming of a city to extend themselves to postures that allow them to kiss the backsides of such people."

Soon, though, there was a move afoot to get another team. Jerry Clinton, who ran Grey Eagle, the Anheuser-Busch distributorship for St. Louis County, was the leader of this movement. He was convinced that the NFL would give St. Louis an expansion team. Clinton would be the owner. Co-owner, actually. His partners were Fran Murray, a flim-flam man from the East Coast, and Walter Payton, a retired football player.

They thought they had their bases covered with the NFL. They had local roots, flim-flammery and a retired football hero who was black. What more did they need?

Well, money.

Yes, these teams cost money. Clinton had some, but not nearly enough, so he looked around and found ... James B. Orthwein.

I was never clear on why Orthwein elected to join Clinton. The partnership seemed doomed from the beginning. It wasn't just that Orthwein was supposed to provide the bulk of the money. The real problem was that his money was Old Money and Clinton's money was New Money.

In some cities, a partnership like that might work, but this city has a caste system as rigid as that of old India. Old Money and New Money don't mix.

And if Orthwein typified Old Money, Clinton typified New Money. Understated and dignified? No way! Clinton was loud, brash and had a "look at me!" attitude. Like a lot of guys who started with nothing, Clinton was darned proud of how far he'd come, and he figured other people were as impressed with his success as he was.

Here was another difference between the two men: Clinton was a former boxer; Orthwein was the master of the hounds at Bridlespur Hunt Club.

At any rate, the partnership fell apart and when Orthwein left, he took his checkbook with him. St. Louis did not get an expansion team.

Orthwein, who briefly owned the New England Patriots during this period, eventually went back to the Hunt Club and the dignity of a life outside the public domain. The preference for such a life must be in the genes. When my colleague, William Lhotka, called one of Orthwein's daughters on Saturday to get some information for an obituary, she said, We don't want anything in the paper. He said, I'm sorry, but I have to write something. Could I have the spelling of your name? No, she said.

As a reporter, I like people who talk to us, but even so, I can appreciate a daughter respecting the wishes of her father. By the way, the funeral service will be private and there will be no memorial service.

COUNTRY CLUBS LOVE A LITTLE SOCIALISM

6.28.2009

To understand the American economic system, which is a hybrid of free enterprise and socialism, you have to understand the difference between a well-struck golf ball at the Tower Tee driving range in Affton and a well-struck golf ball at the St. Louis Country Club in Ladue.

The golf ball at Tower Tee is going to land on property taxed at 32 percent of its appraised value. That is the standard rate for commercial property. The golf ball at St. Louis Country Club is going to land on property taxed at 19 percent of its appraised value. That is the standard rate for residential property.

The golf course at St. Louis Country Club is not really residential. Even in hard times, people don't live on its fairways, or on its greens, or even in its rough. The sort of people who might be so inclined are not welcome. But for tax purposes, golf courses are considered residential.

That's not just country clubs. That's all golf courses. Chapter 137 of the Missouri Revised Statutes declares that the definition of residential property should include "land used as a golf course."

In other words, we subsidize golf courses. Not driving ranges, but golf courses. I'm talking of privately owned golf courses, of course. Municipal golf courses are not taxed.

I am not a golfer, but I have friends who are. Maybe we should subsidize the game. Just don't complain about socialized medicine while on the course. That's all I ask.

But the most interesting aspect is this: A privately owned public course – that is, a course that allows the public to play – faces a higher tax burden than does a private club that excludes the public.

A public course pays the residential rate for the actual golf course but pays the higher commercial rate for other land – the clubhouse, parking lot, swimming pools, tennis courts, outbuildings, etc.

A private club pays the lower residential rate for all its property. That includes its spacious, handsome clubhouse.

This means we're doing more than subsidizing golf. We're subsidizing a lifestyle.

After all, if you go to the corner tavern and order a beer, the price of that beer is going to reflect the taxes the tavern owner pays, and he pays at the commercial rate. Nobody is subsidizing your beer. It's free enterprise and capitalism at the tavern.

But when the country clubber relaxes on the veranda of the clubhouse after a nice round of subsidized golf, the price of his drink reflects the much lower residential rate that the club pays. He gets a subsidized drink. It's socialism at the country club.

Friday morning, I visited Eugene Leung, St. Louis County's director of revenue. I asked if he were a golfer. Not a good one, he said. I said it seems we're subsidizing the country clubbers. Leung is a circumspect man. He said he didn't think of it as subsidizing anybody, but he said the system does seem unfair because the public clubs pay a higher rate than the private clubs. He explained that in 2003, the county reclassified the private clubs to coincide with the public clubs. In other words, the golf courses themselves remained residential, but the clubhouses and restaurants and parking lots and so on were changed to commercial. The private clubs took the county to court and lost, but then won on appeal. The clubs' basic argument was that the public courses were businesses, but the private clubs operate on a not-for-profit basis.

I like that. The St. Louis Country Club. A not-for-profit. Kind of like the Salvation Army or Goodwill.

Besides, maybe we should subsidize our private clubs. A vibrant community needs a robust upper crust. If we're going to attract new businesses, we need clubs for the new bosses to join. What would this region be without the Bogey Club? And let's not turn our backs on the people whose ancestors made fortunes here. What's wrong with our leading families enjoying a subsidized meal now and then at Old Warson?

Some of you are probably thinking that the wealthy ought to pay their own way. But that's not the way of the wealthy. I remember when InBev bought the brewery. According to a filing with the SEC, August Busch IV was due to get $98.95 million plus $120,000 a month. Also, free access to events sponsored by the brewery.

Almost $100 million and he needed free tickets to concerts? That's the way they are.

I'm sure this is not easy on them. I suspect many of them are deeply conflicted. A lot of the folks at St. Louis Country Club are politically conservative. Titans of industry and so on. Talking the conservative talk, living the socialist life.

Maybe now and then, they sneak out to Tower Tee to hit a bucket of balls.

Bill McClellan • Gently Down the Stream

NEIGHBORHOOD'S LONG HISTORY COULD BE OVERWHELMED BY DEVELOPMENT

5.22.2009

Michael Deck came to this country from Germany shortly before the turn of the last century. He married Anna Westerheide, whose family owned a tobacco and cigar store. (That store opened in 1860 and remained open until 2002.)

In 1901, Michael and Anna bought a house in the 1400 block of North Park Place on the city's north side, in a German neighborhood called Bremen. The Decks had nine children – seven sons and two daughters.

The family's life revolved around the nearby Holy Trinity Catholic Church. Not only did the family attend the church, but Deck was a painter who specialized in churches and he did the delicate job of painting the interior of Holy Trinity. Two of the seven sons became priests.

Sometime around 1920, Holy Trinity needed a music director, and the priest contacted a music academy in Regensburg, Germany. Jacob Kremer was the young graduate who came for the job. He was the son of a shoemaker from a small town in the Rhineland.

In 1926, he married Teresa Deck, the youngest of the two Deck daughters. They moved into an apartment just down the street from the Decks. They had six children. Marie was the third.

She grew up surrounded by music. "I can't remember not knowing how to push a piano key down," she told me when I visited her Thursday morning.

Her father died in 1949 while she was in her junior year at St. Elizabeth High School. Shortly thereafter, Marie and her mother moved down the street to the Deck house.

"My grandmother had died by then, and my grandfather would come to our apartment for dinner, and then my mother would go over to his house to clean, and it just didn't make sense," Marie said.

Not surprisingly, Marie became a musician. She played the organ at Holy Trinity – she also briefly taught second grade there – and she earned a bachelor's, a master's and a doctorate at Washington University before earning a Fulbright Scholarship to study in Vienna.

She served as the music director at Holy Cross Church in Baden, and then at St. Monica Catholic Church in West County for 20 years before retiring in 2005.

Except for her stint in Austria, she has always lived in the 1400 block of North Park Place. Over the years, the complexion of the neighborhood changed from all white to mostly black. Interstate 70 slashed through it. Even the name changed – from Bremen to Hyde Park.

Marie has been fine with the changes. She is a friendly person who respects others, and people seem to respect her. From her kitchen window, you can see a crumbling house adjacent to her backyard. It used to be the clubhouse for a motorcycle gang, she told me. She had no problems with them. "Sometimes they'd come over and say, 'Marie, somebody was drinking too much beer and ran into your fence, but don't worry. We'll fix it.' And they would," she said.

But just as there is a crumbling house visible from her kitchen window, there is a renovated house across the street from the crumbling one. "Places like that need to be saved," she said.

The front page of Thursday's newspaper was spread on the kitchen table. It featured a map of Paul McKee's "vision" to develop large swaths of north St. Louis. It appeared that Marie's house – and the block on which she has lived for more than 70 years – was just outside the proposed redevelopment area. Still, the plan could have a huge impact on the neighborhood.

"What do you think?" I asked.

She shrugged. She said it seemed promising, but she worried about people who have spent their lives in north St. Louis. Will they be displaced? Will the city give free rein to McKee? After all, someone could find that it's easier to bulldoze entire blocks rather than knock down one house and save the next.

By the way, Marie's street is lovely. Most of the homes are owner-occupied, and they are well cared for. Just to the east of Marie's home is what seems to be a park. It used to contain a large row house, but that building was demolished, and the space became kind of a dead zone. People pulled cars on the lot to change oil. But Marie and her neighbor on the other side of the lot bought the property themselves and created their own park.

This sort of thing happens. People create gardens, parks, little jewels in unlikely settings. Will a multibillion-dollar plan recognize that? Marie wonders. She worries. As I left, she sat at her organ and began to play. It was something from Bach.

Perhaps she learned it from her father, who married a girl who grew up in the house in which her daughter now lives.

A LETTER, LONG AGO, FOR MISS MILDRED

5.9.2010

After my father died, I began going through boxes of old photographs and papers. These family artifacts had been the domain of my mother. I doubt my dad had ever looked at them.

The photos were the most mysterious. Who were these people? What roles had they played in our family's history? Oh, how I wished I had gone through these photos while my parents were alive.

The papers weren't so mysterious – death certificates, marriage certificates, birth certificates. There was a will from my father in which he left everything to my mother. It was witnessed by Fred Cook, who had been our next-door neighbor.

I remembered when my father wrote that will. Fred, his wife, Dini – a German war bride – and my parents were sitting at the kitchen table drinking. A huge storm was approaching. "I need a will!" said my father. Everyone laughed as he grabbed a pen and paper, speaking the words aloud as he wrote them. "I, Art McClellan, being of sound mind ..."

Amid these papers and photographs I found a letter. It was still in its envelope. It was addressed to Miss Mildred Longton at 515 North Lake Street in Madison, Wis. It was postmarked Dec. 5, 1928. It carried a two-cent stamp. The return address was in Indiana. My mother had spent two years at the University of Wisconsin.

That always seemed a little strange. My mother was from Chicago and did not come from money. Her mother married a streetcar conductor. They had two children – Mildred and Marvin – and then the streetcar conductor left. Neither my mother nor my grandmother, who lived with us, ever spoke of him.

My grandmother supported her two children by working in a candy store. They lived in an apartment on the south side of Chicago. My father was the delivery boy for the local grocery store. He was in high school when he met my mother while delivering groceries to her family's apartment. They did not date.

Then she went to Wisconsin. She returned to Chicago when Marvin graduated from high school. Their mother could only afford to send one child to college, and it was more important for a boy to get an education. Marvin went to the University of Illinois. He flunked out.

I was too self-absorbed to ever ask my mother about Wisconsin. Why had she gone there? What did she want to study? For that matter, what did she think when I flunked out of Illinois? Perhaps it opened old wounds.

At any rate, I knew nothing about that time in her life and now I was looking at an envelope addressed to my mother when she was a coed. I opened it.

"Dearest Mildred: I never thought when I said goodbye that it was so absolutely final. I received a telegram saying that my father was ill, to come home at once. I tried to call, but it was 8 o'clock in the morning and the line was busy. I caught the 9 o'clock train, but it wasn't fast enough, dear. My father is dead. I am all alone.

"Circumstances prevent me from returning to Wisconsin this year and perhaps it will be impossible for me to return at all. I am managing my father's factory and we plan on moving it to Nashville, Tenn., where I have relatives.

"Dearest, I wish I could have said goodbye, but perhaps I would rather keep in my memory that last evening I spent with you, when we walked on the campus together. I hope you cared, a little. Goodbye, Dick."

What was I to make of this?

By itself, the letter didn't suggest a serious relationship. There was no talk of getting together again, not even talk of staying in touch.

But still, my mother had kept that letter. Maybe she sometimes even thought about how life could have been different for her.

The letter made me realize how little I knew of her life before me. That's a thing about mothers. Most of us think of our mothers almost as one-dimensional characters who had no identity until we came along.

In my case, my mom never complained about my self-absorption. If I wanted to think her life started when she became a mother, she wasn't going to tell me differently.

But the letter taught me a lesson.

Years after I read it, my son, who was not yet born when my mother died, decided to go to the University of Wisconsin. The day we took him to school was the first time I had been to Madison.

I took some time and walked past 515 North Lake Street, and I thought not of my mother, but of Miss Mildred Longton. She would, of course, eventually leave that campus, marry the former grocery delivery boy, become my mother and laugh with neighbors as my father wrote a will. But there was a time when she walked on the campus with a young man for whom she might have cared, a little.

ABOUT THE AUTHOR

Bill McClellan grew up in Chicago and attended the University of Illinois. He flunked out, and was drafted into the Marine Corps.

After the Marines, he attended Arizona State University. He was then hired by the Phoenix Gazette. After his girlfriend was accepted into dental school at Washington University, McClellan moved to St. Louis. He was hired by the Post-Dispatch in 1980 and wrote entertainment listings. He then moved to the City Desk where he worked the night city police beat. He began writing a column in 1983.

He and his wife, Mary, who did indeed become a dentist, have two children, Lorna and Jack. Despite her father's admonitions, Lorna attended the University of Illinois. She graduated with a degree in biology. Jack graduated from the University of Wisconsin with a degree in English.

This is McClellan's third collection of columns. He has also written a true-crime book.